THE UNOFFICIAL

SUPER MARIO

COOKBOOK

THE UNOFFICIAL

SUPER MARIO

COOKBOOK

BY
TOM GRIMM

WITH PHOTOS BY
TOM GRIMM & DIMITRIE HARDER

REEL
INK
PRESS

CONTENTS

INTRODUCTION

Super Mario is a phenomenon. The iconic plumber made his first appearance back in 1981, when he faced off against the inimitable Donkey Kong. Soon, he was headlining his own game when *Super Mario Bros.* was released for Nintendo's legendary Famicom game console in 1985. Mario set out to rescue his true love, Princess Peach, from the clutches of his archenemy, Bowser. His adventures catapulted Mario to fame and made *Super Mario* one of the most popular video game series of all time.

With his blue overalls, oversized red cap, and impressive mustache, Mario has been thrilling fans all over the world for over 35 years now—and not just those who steer Mario through fantastic levels packed with memorable creatures and treacherous traps. In fact, there's enough *Super Mario* merchandise out there these days to bring a whole fleet's worth of Bowser's airships down out of the sky: toys, socks, bedding, plushies, magnets, Christmas tree ornaments, lunch boxes, beanbag chairs, remote-controlled cars, shoelaces, bubble bath, comics, animated series, board games, showerheads—and now even a movie, featuring spectacular animation from Illumination, the studio that brought us *Minions*.

But there's one *Super Mario* tie-in that has never been done before: a cookbook!

Mario says, "If food isn't pasta, it doesn't count!" But all the marvelous worlds Mario has jumped in and run through over the decades have a much richer array of culinary delights to add to Italian classics like pasta and pizza (which are also included here, of course). How about a tasty Shroom Steak, Koopasta, Bob-omb Truffles, Bowser's Fire-Charred Corn on the Cob, a piece of Chain Chomp Cake, or Fire Flower Cookies? Who hasn't wondered what would happen if they consumed 1-Up Mushrooms or Ice Power, or what the mysterious Stupendous Stew tastes like? And haven't you always wanted to munch on a Piranha Plant instead of the other way around?

Featuring more than 50 recipes for the whole family to enjoy—including starters, main dishes, sweets, and drinks—this book is sure to offer something for everyone! So what are you waiting for? Trade your plumber's cap and wrench for a chef's hat and wooden spoon, and let's a-cook!

Tom Grimm

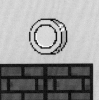

STARTERS

DIFFICULTY: 🍄

YOSHI EGGS

PREP TIME: 5 MINUTES • COOK TIME: 10 MINUTES

SUPER MARIO WORLD (1990) FINDS MARIO, LUIGI, AND PRINCESS PEACH ON YOSHI'S ISLAND. THEY HAD PLANNED A RELAXING VACATION, BUT AS USUAL, BOWSER SHOWS UP TO SPOIL THINGS BY KIDNAPPING PEACH. HE ALSO TRAPS THE YOSHIS LIVING ON THE ISLAND INSIDE EGGS! SO OUR FAVORITE PLUMBER DOES WHAT ANYONE WOULD AND SETS OFF TO RESCUE HIS DARLING AND THE YOSHIS. WITH THIS CUTE, EASY-TO-MAKE APPETIZER, YOU TOO CAN FEEL LIKE YOU'RE EXPLORING THE JUNGLES, MOUNTAINS, AND BREATHTAKING SKIES OF YOSHI'S ISLAND—BUT WITHOUT THE STRESS OF A QUEST!!

★ ★ ★

1. Put the eggs in a large pot and cover them with warm water. Bring to a boil over medium heat, then reduce the heat to maintain a simmer, undisturbed, for 10 minutes. (If you prefer your yolk a bit on the runny side, 8 minutes is enough.) Transfer the eggs to an ice bath and allow to cool for several minutes.

2. Meanwhile, combine the sriracha mayonnaise and green food coloring in a small bowl, adding enough coloring to achieve the desired shade of Yoshi green.

3. Carefully peel the hard-boiled eggs. Use a small brush to dot sriracha mayonnaise all over the eggs so they look like the dots on Yoshi eggs. Allow to dry for several minutes, then serve promptly.

MAKES 6 EGGS

6 eggs

3 tablespoons sriracha mayonnaise

1 to 2 drops green food coloring

TIP If you can't get ready-made sriracha mayonnaise in the supermarket, you can make it at home. In a small bowl, mix ½ cup mayo with 1 to 1½ tablespoons sriracha, 1 teaspoon lemon juice (freshly squeezed is best), 1 minced garlic clove, and salt to taste. Whisk well, then let the sriracha mayonnaise sit in the refrigerator for 30 minutes before using to let the flavors blend.

PIRANHA PLANTS

PREP TIME: 10 MINUTES

PIRANHA PLANTS ARE A REAL NUISANCE. MALICIOUS AS THEY ARE, THEY SNAP AT EVERYTHING THAT CROSSES THEIR PATH—AND THEY REALLY HAVE A TASTE FOR ITALIAN PLUMBERS AND THEIR FRIENDS. TO MAKE MATTERS WORSE, SOME OF THESE VORACIOUS BEASTS CAN EVEN SPIT FIREBALLS! BUT WITH THESE REFRESHINGLY FRUITY APPETIZERS, YOU'LL BE THE ONE DOING THE EATING AFTER ALL THESE YEARS. REVENGE IS SWEET!

★ ★ ★

1. Wash the grapes and strawberries and pat dry with paper towels.

2. Place the strawberries on a cutting board and use a small, sharp knife to cut a mouth-shaped triangle out of each one at the tip end.

3. Depending on their size, stick four to five grapes vertically onto each of 12 skewers, leaving enough free space at the bottom that you can stick the skewer into a half melon that has been flipped over (or something else that can serve as a stand). Top each skewer with a strawberry to create a voracious Piranha Plant.

MAKES 12 SKEWERS

1 pound seedless green grapes

8 ounces fresh strawberries

ALSO REQUIRED

12 long wooden skewers

Stand for skewers (such as half a melon)

MARIO'S MIRACULOUS FIREBALLS

PREP TIME: 75 MINUTES (INCLUDING RESTING) • COOK TIME: 15 MINUTES

BOWSER ISN'T THE ONLY ONE WHO LOVES FLAMES. MARIO LIKES IT HOT FROM TIME TO TIME, TOO—AS LONG AS HE DOESN'T RUN THE RISK OF CATCHING FIRE HIMSELF, THAT IS. SO THESE FIREBALLS ARE JUST RIGHT! THEY PACK QUITE A PUNCH, BUT AT LEAST ENEMIES AREN'T THROWING THEM AT YOU. NOT A FAN OF BREAKING INTO A SWEAT OR HAVING A RUNNY NOSE? THEN TAKE IT EASY ON THE HEAT. WE WOULDN'T WANT YOU TO END UP BREATHING FIRE LIKE MARIO'S ARCHENEMY!

★ ★ ★

TO MAKE THE FIREBALLS:

1. Combine the cheeses, eggs, flour, baking soda, cream of tartar, salt, pepper, cayenne pepper, red pepper flakes, parsley, and oregano in a bowl and, with slightly moistened hands, knead carefully until the ingredients are combined, forming a compact, sticky mass. Cover loosely with plastic wrap and refrigerate for at least 1 hour.

2. Heat about 4 to 5 inches of oil in a large pot over medium heat until the oil reaches 350°F.

3. While the oil is heating, use slightly moistened hands to roll the cheese mass into bite-size balls. Pour the breadcrumbs into a bowl and roll the cheese balls in them until coated. Press the balls slightly into the crumbs to adhere. Add the breaded cheese balls to the hot oil immediately and fry until crisp and golden brown on all sides. The cheese balls are done when they rise to the top on their own (3 to 4 minutes). Use a metal slotted spoon to carefully remove the balls from the oil and place on paper towels on a plate for 2 minutes to drain.

4. Serve warm, with a small bowl of Lighter Fluid Dip.

TO MAKE THE LIGHTER FLUID DIP:

5. Combine the salsa, chili sauce, steak sauce, and sriracha to taste (depending how hot you want your dip) in a small bowl. Mix thoroughly, cover with plastic wrap, and refrigerate until ready to serve. Stir again to combine before serving.

Watch out! You may end up breathing fire.

MAKES 4 SERVINGS

FIREBALLS

3½ cups shredded cheese of your choice

½ cup shredded aged Gouda

½ cup grated Parmesan

2 eggs

2 tablespoons flour

¾ teaspoon baking soda

1½ teaspoon cream of tartar

½ teaspoon salt

¼ teaspoon ground black pepper

½ teaspoon cayenne pepper

½ teaspoon red pepper flakes

1 teaspoon dried parsley

½ teaspoon dried oregano

2 cups oil, for frying

5 tablespoons breadcrumbs

LIGHTER FLUID DIP

5 tablespoons salsa

3 tablespoons chili sauce

2 tablespoons steak sauce

Sriracha, to taste

MUSHROOM AND STAR SALAD

PREP TIME: 5 MINUTES (PLUS 1 HOUR FOR FLAVORS TO MELD) • COOK TIME: 10 MINUTES

IF THERE'S ONE THING THERE'S PLENTY OF IN THE MARIO UNIVERSE—ASIDE FROM DELIGHTFUL FRIENDS AND DASTARDLY ENEMIES—IT'S STARS AND MUSHROOMS. TOUCHING A STAR GIVES MARIO THE POWER OF INVINCIBILITY. EATING MUSHROOMS ALSO GIVES OUR HEROIC PLUMBER SPECIAL POWERS FOR A TIME. STARS AND MUSHROOMS ARE A TRUE POWER-UP—JUST LIKE THIS SALAD, WHICH IS DELICIOUS AND HEALTHY. IT HELPS YOU REFUEL AND RECHARGE SO YOU CAN TACKLE THE NEXT LEVEL!

★ ★ ★

1. Wash the radishes, pat them dry with paper towels, and use a small, sharp knife to slice off a few flat round pieces on all sides, leaving the radishes with large white circles across the surface so they look like Super Mushrooms.

2. Clean the mushrooms, remove and discard the stems, and slice the caps as you prefer.

3. Combine the vinegar, sugar, and 1 tablespoon of the olive oil in a small bowl. Chop the lemon balm and stir in. Cover the dressing loosely with plastic wrap and refrigerate for 1 hour to allow the flavors to meld.

4. Meanwhile, heat the remaining 1 tablespoon of olive oil in a small frying pan over medium heat. Add the onion and sweat until translucent. Add the mushrooms, stir well to combine, and sauté on all sides for 3 to 4 minutes. Remove from the heat and drain the excess liquid.

5. Transfer the salad, star fruit, radishes, and sautéed mushrooms and onions to a large bowl. Toss with the dressing until evenly coated. Divide among three bowls and sprinkle to taste with pine nuts and parsley. Serve immediately.

MAKES 3 SERVINGS

½ bunch radishes (about 18)

14 ounces mixed mushrooms

2 tablespoons raspberry vinegar

1 teaspoon sugar

2 tablespoons olive oil, divided

2 sprigs fresh lemon balm

1 small red onion, diced

7 ounces mixed salad

1 star fruit, thinly sliced

Pine nuts, for garnish

Minced fresh parsley, for garnish

DRY BONES ONIGIRI

PREP TIME: 20 MINUTES • COOK TIME: 50 MINUTES

DRY BONES ARE SKELETAL VERSIONS OF KOOPA TROOPAS. THEY ARE SOME OF THE STRONGEST ENEMIES IN THE MARIO UNIVERSE. THEY CAN REGENERATE, ARE IMPERVIOUS TO FIRE, AND HANG AROUND DARK, CREEPY PLACES, OFTEN GETTING UP TO NO GOOD WITH BOOS. HERE, BY CONTRAST, THEY ARE THE STARS OF THE SHOW IN THE FORM OF THESE ONIGIRI—WHICH, BY THE WAY, ARE ANYTHING BUT BONE DRY. THEY'RE SOFT AND STICKY, AND PRETTY DARN SAVORY TO BOOT!

★ ★ ★

1. Put the rice in a strainer and rinse under cold running water until the runoff is no longer cloudy, but clear.

2. Transfer the rice to a medium pot and add enough water to fully cover the rice (about 1½ cups). Allow to stand for 15 minutes.

3. Turn on the stove and bring the rice to a boil over medium heat. Then adjust the heat to low, cover, and simmer the rice, stirring occasionally (so it does not burn and stick to the pan), for about 20 minutes, or until the water has completely evaporated. Then remove the lid and allow to rest for 5 minutes.

4. Stir the vinegar, salt, and sugar into the rice and allow to stand for another 5 minutes.

5. Use scissors to cut the nori sheets into pieces that fit under your bone-shaped cookie cutter, then set the cookie cutter over the piece of nori and press rice into it, packing firmly so the rice maintains its shape. Carefully press the rice out of the cookie cutter and sprinkle with furikake to taste. Serve immediately.

MAKES 20 PIECES

2½ cups sushi rice

3 tablespoons plus 1 teaspoon rice wine vinegar

2 teaspoons salt

1 teaspoon sugar

1 to 2 nori sheets

Furikake (Japanese seasoning blend), for topping

ALSO REQUIRED

Bone-shaped cookie cutter

DIFFICULTY: 🍄

BOWSER'S FIRE-CHARRED CORN ON THE COB

PREP TIME: 10 MINUTES • COOK TIME: 25 MINUTES

WATCH OUT! BOWSER IS THE SUPREME LEADER OF THE KOOPA TROOP, THE FATHER OF BOWSER JR., AND MARIO'S SWORN ENEMY. HIS ONE DESIRE IS TO REIGN SUPREME OVER THE MUSHROOM KINGDOM. AND FOR THE LIFE OF HIM, HE JUST CAN'T STOP KIDNAPPING MARIO'S DARLING PRINCESS PEACH, WHOM HE SIMPLY MUST MARRY—WHETHER SHE WANTS TO OR NOT. BUT THERE'S ONE THING BOWSER LOVES ALMOST AS MUCH AS THE LOVELY PRINCESS: FIRE! THIS JUICY, SWEET CORN ON THE COB WITH ULTRA-SPICY SAUCE IS RIGHT UP HIS ALLEY!

★ ★ ★

TO MAKE THE CORN ON THE COB:

1. Over medium heat, bring a large pot of water to a boil. Add the corn, milk, and sugar. Cover and cook the corn for 8 to 10 minutes. While the corn is cooking, prepare the Chile Mayonnaise.

2. Turn on your oven's broiler. Line a baking sheet with parchment paper.

3. Take the corn out of the water and drain thoroughly. Carefully insert the corn holders into each end of the cob. Brush the melted butter on all sides of the corn and place each cob on the baking sheet. Place the baking sheet on the top rack and broil for 5 to 6 minutes, turning regularly and brushing butter drippings from the pan back over the corn. If you really want your corn to be Bowser-style, leave it to broil for 3 to 4 minutes more, until charred.

4. Remove the pan from the oven and allow to cool briefly.

TO MAKE THE CHILE MAYONNAISE:

5. Separate the eggs; all you need is the yolks.

6. Combine the yolks and mustard in a bowl. Season to taste with salt and pepper. Then, using an electric mixer with a whisk attachment, beat constantly on medium speed. Add the oil drop by drop until the mayonnaise begins to bind. Then pour in the rest of the oil in a thin stream and carefully combine. Be careful not to overmix the mayonnaise, or it will break!

7. Season to taste with sriracha, lemon juice, a bit more salt, and diced chiles to taste (depending on how spicy you want it). Refrigerate until ready to serve.

8. Serve corn immediately with the Chile Mayonnaise on the side for slathering the corn.

MAKES 4 SERVINGS

CORN ON THE COB

4 cobs sweet corn

⅜ cup milk

1 tablespoon sugar

¼ cup melted butter, to coat

CHILE MAYONNAISE

2 egg yolks

1 teaspoon mustard

Salt

Ground black pepper

1 cup sunflower oil

2 tablespoons sriracha sauce

Juice of 1 lemon

1 to 2 red chiles, minced

ALSO REQUIRED

8 corn holders

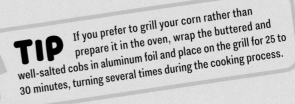

TIP If you prefer to grill your corn rather than prepare it in the oven, wrap the buttered and well-salted cobs in aluminum foil and place on the grill for 25 to 30 minutes, turning several times during the cooking process.

21

BIRDO'S CHICKEN DRUMSTICKS

PREP TIME: 5 MINUTES (PLUS AT LEAST 3 HOURS TO MARINATE) • COOK TIME: 30 MINUTES

BIRDO IS A SMALL, PINK DINOSAUR WITH A HUGE RED BOW AND THE ABILITY TO SHOOT EGGS FROM HER MOUTH. WHILE SHE WAS ONE OF THE BOSSES IN *SUPER MARIO BROS. 2* (1988), SHE'S NOW FIRMLY PART OF THE MARIO CLIQUE. AND SHE LOVES BEING A PART OF THE CREW! WHETHER GOLFING WITH THE OTHERS, PUTTING ON THEATRICAL PERFORMANCES, OR SINGING IN MUSIC FESTIVALS, BIRDO PASSIONATELY ENJOYS HER FAVORITE THINGS: THE SPOTLIGHT, BIG RED BOWS, SPARKLY THINGS, AND HER DEAR FRIENDS.

★ ★ ★

1. Combine the honey, soy sauce, and sweet-and-sour sauce in a small bowl. Add the chile, ginger, and garlic and combine.

2. Rinse the chicken legs with water and pat dry with paper towels. Transfer the chicken to a large freezer bag and pour the marinade over it. Carefully massage the marinade into the meat, then refrigerate for at least 3 hours.

3. Preheat the oven to 400°F. Line a baking sheet with parchment paper.

4. Remove the marinated chicken legs and set them on the prepared baking sheet, leaving space between them. Transfer the remaining marinade to a small bowl.

5. Roast the chicken for 25 to 30 minutes until golden brown, turning every 5 minutes and generously brushing with the remaining marinade the first two times you turn.

6. Remove the chicken from the oven and sprinkle with the black sesame seeds. Serve promptly with a small bowl of Lighter Fluid Dip.

MAKES 4 SERVINGS

3 tablespoons honey

½ cup soy sauce

½ cup sweet-and-sour sauce

1 red chile, minced

1 piece ginger root (a little over 1 inch), peeled and minced

6 garlic cloves, minced

8 chicken legs

2 teaspoons black sesame seeds

Lighter Fluid Dip (see page 15), for serving

MARIO HATS

PREP TIME: 15 MINUTES

WHERE WOULD MARIO BE WITHOUT THE MANY HELPERS ACCOMPANYING HIM ON HIS ADVENTURES, AS WELL AS HIS SIGNATURE RED HAT? CAPPY, A BONNETER FROM CAP KINGDOM, WAS BOTH MARIO'S HELPER AND HIS RED HAT! HE JOINED MARIO IN *SUPER MARIO ODYSSEY* (2017) TO HELP HIM RESCUE HIS SISTER TIARA AND PRINCESS PEACH, WHO HAS BEEN KIDNAPPED BY THE DASTARDLY BOWSER YET AGAIN. HERE, WE'RE PAYING SPECIAL TRIBUTE TO THIS ICONIC RED HAT IN SNACK FORM—BUT IF YOU WANT, YOU CAN COLOR SOME OF THE MAYONNAISE RED AND BLACK WITH FOOD COLORING AND PIPE A PAIR OF EYES TO CREATE CAPPY. WHETHER YOU'RE SHOWING OFF THE SIGNATURE HAT OR CAPPY HIMSELF, YOUR GUESTS WILL BE JUST AS AMAZED AS YOU WERE WHEN YOU FIRST WALKED THROUGH CITYLAND!

★ ★ ★

1. Carefully open three of the cheese snacks and remove the cheese from the red wax coating. Carefully cut the coatings in half horizontally on the counter, then use a small, sharp knife to cut a half-moon-shaped bill for Mario's hat out of each of the six small wax disks.

2. Place the mayonnaise in a pastry bag with a fine piping tip attached. (If you don't happen to have a pastry bag handy, you can also use a freezer bag with one corner cut off.) Pipe an "M" shape on the side of each cheese still coated with wax and allow to dry for several minutes.

3. Place a drop of edible glue on the back of each cut-out "wax bill" and place the decorated cheese snacks on top so the whole thing looks like Mario's hat. Press gently into place until the glue sticks and store in a container with an airtight seal until ready to serve.

MAKES 6 HATS

9 wax-wrapped cheese snacks

2 to 3 teaspoons mayonnaise

Edible glue

ALSO REQUIRED

Pastry bag and fine tip

TIP You can either polish off the three peeled cheese snacks right away or use them to make other dishes featured in this book, such as Mona Pizza's Megapizza (see page 49).

VEGGIE TOADS

PREP TIME: 70 MINUTES (INCLUDING RISING TIME) • COOK TIME: 20 MINUTES

TOADS ARE EVERYWHERE IN THE MUSHROOM KINGDOM! THEY GUARD AND SERVE IN PEACH'S CASTLE, RUN STORES AND OTHER ESTABLISHMENTS IN TOAD TOWN, AND EVEN SOMETIMES GO OUT ON ADVENTURES LIKE THE TOAD BRIGADE! WE HAD TO HONOR THESE HELPFUL, PEACEFUL FRIENDS WITH A DELICIOUS MUFFIN RECIPE. JUST LIKE THESE DEPENDABLE FRIENDS, THIS VEGGIE-FILLED SNACK WILL WARM YOUR HEART AND SOUL.

★ ★ ★

TO MAKE THE YEAST DOUGH:

1. Sift the flour into a large bowl and make a hollow in the middle. Add the yeast and sugar. Pour the water into the hollow and use an electric mixer or a stand mixer with a dough hook attachment to roughly combine for 1 minute on the lowest setting. Then cover the bowl with a clean dish cloth and set in a warm place to rise for at least 30 minutes, or until it has nearly doubled in volume.

2. As soon as the dough has risen, add the salt and oil and use your hands to knead into a smooth dough (about 5 to 8 minutes). Cover and allow to rise in a warm place for another 30 minutes.

TO MAKE THE FILLING:

3. Meanwhile, combine the zucchini, carrot, and pesto in a bowl. Season to taste with salt and pepper.

4. Use a ¾-inch cookie cutter to cut 50 small circles out of the cheese slices. Finely chop the leftover cheese and mix it in with the vegetables and pesto.

TO ASSEMBLE:

5. Preheat the oven to 350°F. Grease a muffin pan.

6. Knead the dough vigorously on a lightly floured surface for about 5 minutes and divide it into 24 pieces of equal size.

7. Place one piece of dough in the bottom of each muffin tin and press gently into place on all sides. Then center a heaping teaspoon of filling on top of the first piece of dough, set a second piece of dough on top, and press into place, making sure the dough sticks up over the top of each muffin cup so it looks like the top of a mushroom. Bake for 15 to 20 minutes, or until golden.

8. Meanwhile, combine the tomato paste with 1 tablespoon of water and do the same with the pesto.

9. Take the muffins out of the oven. Brush half of the "mushroom caps" with the pesto and the other half with tomato paste. Garnish each muffin with three to four cheese circles and leave in the muffin pan to cool completely. Then carefully remove and use a black edible marker to draw two small vertical lines for the eyes (see image).

MAKES 12 TOADS

YEAST DOUGH

3⅓ cups flour, plus more for the counter

2 packets (4½ teaspoons) active dry yeast

1 tablespoon sugar

1 cup lukewarm water

½ teaspoon salt

2 tablespoons olive oil

FILLING

1 zucchini, finely grated

1 carrot, finely grated

3.5 ounces green pesto

Salt

Ground black pepper

7 ounces sliced cheese of choice

ASSEMBLY

2 tablespoons tomato paste

2 tablespoons water, divided

3.5 ounces green pesto

ALSO REQUIRED

Black edible marker

Muffin pan

Small round cookie cutter (about ¾ inch in diameter)

TOASTED BRICK BLOCKS

PREP TIME: 3 MINUTES • COOK TIME: 10 MINUTES

BRICK BLOCKS ARE EVERYWHERE IN THE MUSHROOM KINGDOM, AND THEY'RE VERY DIFFERENT FROM THE MANY OTHER KINDS OF BLOCKS, SINCE THEY ALMOST NEVER HIDE ANY OTHER ITEMS (OTHER THAN THE OCCASIONAL SHOWER OF COINS). BRICK BLOCKS ARE ALSO PRACTICALLY INDESTRUCTIBLE, AND EVEN IF YOU DO MANAGE TO SMASH THEM, THE FRAGMENTS ARE SURE TO BE INEDIBLE—UNLIKE THESE HEARTY SANDWICHES FILLED WITH CHEESE, SALAMI, AND HAM. FEEL FREE TO ADD A LETTUCE LEAF TO MAKE IT HEALTHIER IF YOU'D LIKE, BUT HONESTLY, WITH FLAVOR LIKE THIS, YOU WON'T MISS IT!

★ ★ ★

1. Prepare a sandwich toaster according to the toaster instructions, preheating as necessary. If necessary, brush with a thin coat of butter.

2. Lightly butter one side of each slice of bread. Top two of the slices with the salami, ham, and cheese, then neatly top with the other slices of bread, butter side up.

3. Toast according to the toaster instructions (typically 6 to 8 minutes), or until the sandwich is browned as desired and the cheese is nice and melted. Serve immediately.

MAKES 2 SERVINGS

Butter, for the bread

4 slices bread

2 large slices or 4 small slices salami

2 slices ham

2 large slices cheese of choice

ALSO REQUIRED

Sandwich toaster (ideally with brick pattern)

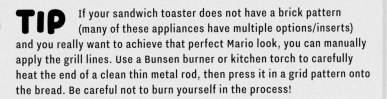

TIP If your sandwich toaster does not have a brick pattern (many of these appliances have multiple options/inserts) and you really want to achieve that perfect Mario look, you can manually apply the grill lines. Use a Bunsen burner or kitchen torch to carefully heat the end of a clean thin metal rod, then press it in a grid pattern onto the bread. Be careful not to burn yourself in the process!

FIRE FLOWERS

PREP TIME: 20 MINUTES

MUNCHING ON VEGGIES IS ALL THE RAGE IN THE MUSHROOM KINGDOM. AND NO WONDER!
THE FIRE FLOWERS THAT GROW THERE GIVE MARIO THE TEMPORARY POWER TO SHOOT FIREBALLS
OUT OF HIS HANDS. THESE APPETIZERS DON'T DO ANYTHING QUITE SO SPECTACULAR,
BUT YOU'RE SURE TO HEAR PLENTY OF OOHS AND AAHS IF YOU SERVE THESE EASY-TO-MAKE
FIRE FLOWERS AT YOUR NEXT MARIO PARTY!

★ ★ ★

1. Cut the cheese into bite-size cubes (about 1¼ inches on each side) and place them on a serving plate, leaving space between them.

2. Wash the cucumber, dry it carefully, and slice it crosswise into ½-inch-thick disks. Use a 1¼-inch cookie cutter (or the thick end of a cake decorating tip) to cut the middle out of each slice of cucumber. Then cut the slices of cucumber in half horizontally.

3. Wash and dry the carrot. Leaving the peel on, slice the carrot into ½-inch-thick disks. Then use a small, sharp knife to carefully cut two small triangles out of one side to produce a flame shape (see image).

4. Poke a toothpick through each cucumber "leaf," inserting the toothpick so it sticks out far enough at the bottom to be stuck into one of the cubes of cheese. Then place one of the carrot "flames" on top of each toothpick, leaving enough room between it and the cucumber that the resulting appetizer looks like a flower.

MAKES 6 SERVINGS

10-ounce block of your desired cheese

1 cucumber

1 large carrot

ALSO REQUIRED

20 toothpicks

1¼-inch round cookie cutter

BOWSER'S FIERY BREATH

PREP TIME: 40 MINUTES (PLUS 3–4 WEEKS TO FERMENT KIMCHI AND AT LEAST 6 HOURS TO MARINATE CHICKEN) • COOK TIME: 30 MINUTES

BOWSER IS ONE OF THE STRONGEST ENEMIES IN THE MUSHROOM KINGDOM. EVEN MARIO HIMSELF SOMETIMES HAS A HARD TIME BEATING HIM. ONE OF THE MOST DANGEROUS WEAPONS IN BOWSER'S ARSENAL IS HIS DREADED FIERY BREATH. THIS SANDWICH BRINGS A SIMILAR HEAT, SO YOU MIGHT THINK OF IT AS THE FINAL BOSS OF THIS CHAPTER. IF YOU DON'T PLAN ON BREATHING FIRE YOURSELF, TRY DIALING DOWN THE HEAT TO TASTE. DON'T WORRY, NO ONE WILL THINK LESS OF YOU FOR IT! (EXCEPT BOWSER, PERHAPS . . .)

★ ★ ★

TO MAKE THE KIMCHI:

1. Use a large, sharp knife to quarter the cabbage, then cut out the core and cut the cabbage into bite-size pieces. Place in a large bowl. Add the carrot, scallions, and radish. Then add the salt. Combine thoroughly and gently knead the salt into the vegetables so they release liquid and stand in their own juices.

2. Use a food processor to finely purée the garlic, ginger, onion, apple, chili powder, cayenne pepper, sugar, and fish sauce. If the purée is too thick, add water.

3. Pour the sauce into the bowl containing the vegetables and combine, ensuring that the cabbage is coated with the seasoning on all sides. Then layer the kimchi into mason jars that have been rinsed with hot water (or, alternatively, place in freezer bags), pressing down firmly on each layer. Leave about 1¼ inches of room at the top so the kimchi does not spill over during fermentation. Make sure the cabbage is fully covered with liquid in the jar and there are no air bubbles in it. (Glass fermentation weights are perfect for this.)

4. Carefully close the jars and leave at room temperature for five to seven days to ferment. After that, refrigerate for two to three weeks, tasting occasionally to see whether the kimchi is as you like it. The longer the kimchi ferments, the stronger and more aromatic it becomes.

MAKES 6 SERVINGS

KIMCHI

½ napa cabbage (about 2 pounds)

1 small carrot, peeled and finely grated or julienned

1 bunch scallions, thinly sliced into rings

1 small daikon radish, finely grated or julienned

2 tablespoons salt

2 garlic cloves, coarsely chopped

1 piece fresh ginger root (about 2 inches), peeled and coarsely chopped

1 small onion, coarsely chopped

½ sweet apple, finely grated or julienned

2 tablespoons chili powder

2 teaspoons cayenne pepper

1 teaspoon sugar

1 tablespoon fish sauce

FRIED CHICKEN

1.75 pounds boneless skinless chicken breast

3 tablespoons paprika

2 tablespoons sea salt

2 tablespoons ground black pepper

2 tablespoons chili powder

1 tablespoon garlic powder

1 tablespoon onion powder

1 tablespoon turbinado or raw sugar

4 cups buttermilk

1⅓ cups milk

2 eggs

1¾ cups breadcrumbs

¾ cup plus 4 teaspoons flour

8 to 9 cups corn flakes, crushed

2 to 3 quarts (64 to 96 fluid ounces) peanut oil, for frying

ASSEMBLY

6 French rolls

1 small red chile, thinly sliced into rings

Red pepper flakes, for topping

Sweet-and-sour sauce, for topping

ALSO REQUIRED

2 to 3 glass jars with lids

Continued on page 32

Continued from page 31

5. Kimchi will keep, sealed, in the refrigerator for several months.

TO MAKE THE FRIED CHICKEN:

6. Place the chicken in a large bowl. Add the paprika, sea salt, pepper, chili powder, garlic powder, onion powder, and sugar. Vigorously massage the seasoning into the meat and spread evenly around the surface. Cover completely with the buttermilk and marinate in the refrigerator for at least 6 hours (ideally overnight).

7. Combine the milk and eggs in a shallow bowl. In a separate shallow bowl, combine the breadcrumbs, flour, and corn flakes.

8. Remove the chicken from the marinade and immerse directly into the milk mixture, coating evenly. Then dredge in the breadcrumb mixture so the meat is thickly coated on all sides. Set the breaded chicken on a plate, repeating until all of the meat is breaded. Dispose of the marinade.

9. Heat the peanut oil in a large pot until it reaches 350°F. Line a baking sheet with parchment paper. Place a rack on the baking sheet and preheat the oven to 175°F.

10. Fry the chicken in batches (being careful not to overcrowd the pot), turning repeatedly to cook all sides, for about 10 to 12 minutes until golden brown and cooked through. Set the fried chicken on the rack in the preheated oven so it will keep warm until it is served and the excess oil can drain off.

TO ASSEMBLE:

11. Cut the French rolls open, leaving a small "hinge" connecting the top and bottom halves. If desired, toast the rolls slightly. Then spread an even layer of kimchi on the bottom half of each roll and set a few pieces of fried chicken on top. If you really want to copy Bowser and breathe fire, garnish with the chile, sprinkle with a pinch of red pepper flakes, and drizzle with sweet-and-sour sauce. Serve immediately.

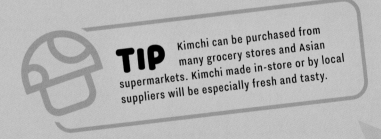

TIP Kimchi can be purchased from many grocery stores and Asian supermarkets. Kimchi made in-store or by local suppliers will be especially fresh and tasty.

MAINS

YUMMY MEAL

PREP TIME: 10 MINUTES • COOK TIME: 30 MINUTES

EVER SINCE *PAPER MARIO* WAS RELEASED BACK IN 2001, FANS HAVE WONDERED WHAT LIES UNDER THE SILVER CLOCHE YOU GET WHEN YOU COMBINE ITEMS SUCH AS ULTRA SHROOMS AND FIRE FLOWERS, DRIED FRUIT AND ICED POTATOES, OR POTATO SALAD AND SPAGHETTI. AFTER MORE THAN 20 YEARS OF WILD SPECULATION, WE'LL LET YOU IN ON THE SECRET RIGHT HERE. DRUMROLL! UNDER THE CLOCHE IS—SURPRISE!—MARIO HIMSELF! IN TWO DIFFERENT FLAVORS!

★ ★ ★

MAKES 2–3 SERVINGS

BUTTERED RICE

1 cup basmati or jasmine rice

1½ cups water

1 teaspoon salt

2 tablespoons butter

TOMATO RICE

1 cup long-grain rice

1½ cups water

1 tablespoon olive oil

1 small onion, diced

1 garlic clove, pressed

2 tablespoons tomato paste

½ teaspoon sugar

7 ounces tomato purée

1 teaspoon vegetable bouillon powder

1 teaspoon gyros seasoning blend

Ground black pepper

ASSEMBLY

1 hard-boiled egg

1 nori sheet

1 black olive, halved horizontally

TO MAKE THE BUTTERED RICE:

1. Combine the rice and water in a medium pot. Add the salt and allow to soften for 10 minutes.

2. Bring the rice to a boil over medium heat. Immediately adjust the heat to low, cover, and cook for 12 to 15 minutes, or until all the water has been absorbed. Do not stir.

3. Remove the rice from the heat and add the butter to melt. Combine thoroughly so the butter is nicely distributed throughout the rice.

TO MAKE THE TOMATO RICE:

4. Combine the rice and water in a medium pot. Bring to a boil over medium heat. Immediately adjust the heat to low, cover, and cook for 12 to 15 minutes, or until all the water has been absorbed, stirring occasionally with a wooden spoon so the rice does not burn and stick to the pan.

5. Meanwhile, heat the olive oil in a small pot over medium heat. Add the onion and sweat for 3 minutes, until translucent. Stir in the garlic and tomato paste and sauté for 1 minute. Add the sugar, tomato purée, and bouillon powder, combine thoroughly, and cook for 10 minutes to reduce, stirring frequently. Add the gyros seasoning and season to taste with pepper.

6. Add the cooked rice to the sauce and combine thoroughly until the rice is red and smooth.

TO ASSEMBLE:

7. Thinly slice the hard-boiled egg vertically. Use kitchen shears to cut the elements needed for Mario's mustache and eyebrows out of the nori sheet (see image).

8. Using your fingers, shape Mario's head out of the white rice on a large serving plate. Add the ears and button nose. Then use the tomato rice to create his cap. Use the egg slices to place the eyes on the face. Set the black olive halves on the egg "eyes" to make "pupils." Finally, place the cut nori elements on top to create the mustache and eyebrows. Serve warm.

GREEN SHELLS

PREP TIME: 30 MINUTES • COOK TIME: 20 MINUTES

KOOPA SHELLS ARE ALMOST AS OLD AS THE MARIO FRANCHISE ITSELF. OFTEN USED AS PROJECTILES, KOOPA SHELLS CAN NOW ALSO BE EATEN TO GAIN VARIOUS ABILITIES. A RED SHELL, FOR EXAMPLE, LETS YOSHI SPIT FIREBALLS, WHILE EATING A BLUE SHELL GIVES YOSHI WINGS FOR A TIME. THIS GREEN KOOPA SHELL CALZONE, BY CONTRAST, IS NOTHING BUT DELICIOUS. IT'S FILLED WITH HEARTY CHEESE AND YAKISOBA, A TRADITIONAL JAPANESE NOODLE DISH.

★ ★ ★

1. Cook the soba noodles according to the package instructions, usually boiling for about 6 minutes. Drain, transfer to a medium bowl, and use kitchen shears to cut the cooked noodles into smaller pieces (about 2 to 3 inches).

2. Preheat the oven to 350°F. Line a baking sheet with parchment paper.

3. In a small bowl, combine the Worcestershire sauce, oyster sauce, soy sauce, and sugar and stir until the sugar has dissolved completely. Then pour this mixture over the noodles, combine carefully, and allow to stand for several minutes to allow the flavors to meld. Season to taste with more of the Worcestershire, oyster, and soy sauces.

4. Roll out the pizza dough on a counter and use a 3- to 4-inch glass to cut out 24 circles.

5. Working with one circle of dough at a time, place a piece of dough in the palm of your hand, press a mozzarella ball into the middle, and set about 1 tablespoon of soba noodles on top. Cover with a second piece of dough and seal securely, pressing the edges together with the tips of your fingers. Set on the prepared baking sheet. Repeat with the remaining dough, mozzarella, and noodles.

6. Combine the wasabi paste and a very small amount of water in a small bowl and use a pastry brush to apply a turtle-like pattern reminiscent of a Koopa shell to the top half of each calzone (see image).

7. Bake for 10 to 12 minutes. Serve promptly.

MAKES 12 SHELLS

10.5 ounces soba noodles

3 tablespoons Worcestershire sauce

2 teaspoons oyster sauce

2 teaspoons soy sauce

1 teaspoon sugar

1.75 pounds ready-made pizza dough

12 mini mozzarella balls

4 tablespoons wasabi paste

ROSALINA'S SUPER STAR TERIYAKI

PREP TIME: 10 MINUTES • COOK TIME: 25 MINUTES

ROSALINA WATCHES OVER THE COSMOS FROM HER OBSERVATORY AND IS THE LOVING ADOPTIVE MOTHER OF THE LUMAS, STAR-LIKE CREATURES WITH THE ABILITY TO TRANSFORM INTO ENTIRE GALAXIES. ROSALINA AND HER LUMAS HELP MARIO AND HIS FRIENDS WHENEVER THEY CAN. THAT'S WHY THIS DELICIOUS DISH IS DEDICATED TO THEM!

★ ★ ★

1. Combine soy sauce, teriyaki sauce, sweet-and-sour sauce, sesame oil, honey, garlic, ginger, and cornstarch in a small bowl.

2. Put the rice in a strainer and rinse in cold running water until the runoff no longer looks cloudy. Then add the rice, 1 teaspoon of salt, and 1½ cups water to a medium pot and bring to a boil over medium heat. Adjust the heat to low, cover, and cook for 12 to 15 minutes, or until all the water has been absorbed.

3. While the rice is cooking, place the olive oil in a frying pan and heat over medium heat. As soon as the oil is hot, add the chicken to the pan and sear about 10 minutes, stirring constantly, or until the meat is golden brown and cooked through. Season to taste with salt and pepper, then deglaze the pan with the prepared sauce. Cook, uncovered, for an additional 5 to 7 minutes, or until the sauce has thickened noticeably.

4. Meanwhile, remove the cooked rice from the heat and stir in the turmeric. Press the rice into a large star-shaped cookie cutter to create a star of rice on each plate, then garnish each star with two pieces of black olive for the eyes. Arrange the teriyaki chicken next to the rice, then sprinkle with the toasted sesame seeds and scallion. Serve immediately.

MAKES 2 SERVINGS

2 tablespoons soy sauce

5 tablespoons teriyaki sauce

2 tablespoons sweet-and-sour sauce

1 teaspoon sesame oil

1½ tablespoons honey

2 garlic cloves, pressed

1 small piece ginger root, peeled and minced

2 teaspoons cornstarch

1 cup rice

1 teaspoon salt

1 tablespoon olive oil

1 pound boneless skinless chicken, cut into bite-size pieces

Salt

Ground black pepper

1 teaspoon turmeric

4 small pieces black olive, cut lengthwise

1 teaspoon toasted sesame seeds

½ scallion, green part only, thinly sliced

ALSO REQUIRED

Large star-shaped cookie cutter

YOSHI CARBONARA

PREP TIME: 5 MINUTES • COOK TIME: 15 MINUTES

YOSHIS ARE FRIENDLY, PEACE-LOVING BEINGS WHO FIRST APPEARED IN *SUPER MARIO WORLD* (1990). THE MOST FAMOUS YOSHI OF ALL, OF COURSE, IS YOSHI HIMSELF. SMALL, GREEN, AND CUDDLY, WITH A SUPER-POWERED TONGUE AND FLUTTERING FLIGHT, YOSHI IS A CREATURE OF MANY TALENTS—MUCH LIKE THIS VERSATILE SPINACH SPAGHETTI DISH, COOKED UP WITH PRIDE IN HONOR OF EVERYONE'S FAVORITE YOSHI!

★ ★ ★

1. Boil the spaghetti in a large pot of generously salted water, following the package directions, until it is al dente.

2. While the spaghetti is cooking, heat the olive oil in a frying pan over medium heat. Add the shallots and garlic and sweat until translucent (3 to 4 minutes). Add the pancetta and sauté until crisp on all sides. Add the baby spinach and combine. Adjust the heat to low, cover, and continue to cook for 2 to 3 minutes.

3. Whisk the heavy cream, Parmesan, and eggs together in a small bowl.

4. Drain the cooked spaghetti and add the pasta to the pan. Transfer the cream mixture to the pan, combine carefully, and heat briefly until the sauce thickens. Season with salt and pepper and divide between two plates. Place small "piles" of spinach on top of the pasta so they look like the green spots on Yoshi eggs.

MAKES 2 SERVINGS

5.5 ounces spaghetti

Salt

1 tablespoon olive oil

2 shallots, minced

1 garlic clove, minced

5.5 ounces pancetta, diced

14 ounces baby spinach

1 cup heavy cream

1.5 ounces Parmesan, freshly grated

2 eggs

Ground black pepper

SHY GYŪDON

PREP TIME: 5 MINUTES • COOK TIME: 30 MINUTES

ALTHOUGH SHY GUYS OCCASIONALLY HELP MARIO AND HIS FRIENDS DURING THEIR ADVENTURES, NO ONE REALLY KNOWS WHAT'S BEHIND THEIR MASKS. WHAT WE DO KNOW IS THAT GYŪDON IS A POPULAR JAPANESE RICE DISH WITH BEEF AND ONIONS. THE RED PICKLED GINGER IN THIS RECIPE IS A NOD TO THE ICONIC ROBES WORN BY THE PINT-SIZE MASKED MEN.

★ ★ ★

1. Put the rice in a strainer and rinse under cold running water until the runoff is no longer cloudy, but clear.

2. Transfer the rice to a pot and add 2½ cups water. Cover and bring to a boil over high heat. Immediately adjust the heat to low and simmer for 15 to 20 minutes, stirring occasionally, until all of the liquid has been absorbed.

3. While the rice is cooking, quarter the onion and break it into its individual layers.

4. Combine the dashi, sugar, sake, soy sauce, ginger juice, and mirin in a small bowl.

5. Heat the oil in a frying pan over medium heat and sweat the onions until they are translucent. Then add the beef and brown on all sides for 2 to 3 minutes. Add the sauce and stir well to combine. Bring to a boil and simmer for 5 minutes, or until the meat is done and the sauce has thickened considerably.

6. Divide the cooked rice between two bowls and top with beef and sauce to taste. Sprinkle with the scallion and a bit of toasted sesame seeds and serve garnished with pickled ginger.

MAKES 2 SERVINGS

1½ cups short-grain rice

1 large onion

1 tablespoon vegetable oil

1¼ cups dashi

3 tablespoons sugar

2 tablespoons sake

4 tablespoons soy sauce

2 tablespoons ginger juice

2 tablespoons mirin

9 ounces beef, thinly sliced and then cut into bite-size pieces

1 scallion, thinly sliced into rings

Toasted sesame seeds

Pickled red ginger

TIP If ready-pickled red ginger isn't available in your supermarket, you can pickle it at home. However, you must do this a week in advance so the ginger has time to ferment.

For 4 servings of pickled red ginger, you need 1 cup fresh ginger, 2 tablespoons salt, ½ cup rice vinegar, and 2 tablespoons sugar. Peel the ginger and cut it into thin slices (preferably with a vegetable slicer). Spread the ginger slices on a surface lined with parchment paper, sprinkle evenly with the salt, and let them sit for an hour. Once the hour is up, bring some water to a boil in a small saucepan and blanch the ginger briefly (about 2 to 3 minutes). Pack the ginger tightly down into hot, rinsed, sealable jars. Bring the vinegar and sugar to boil in a saucepan, stirring constantly, and boil briefly. Pour the brine over the ginger, filling the jar to within ½ inch of the top. Close tightly and allow to infuse for at least a week, shaking occasionally. Stored in a dark, cool place, red ginger will keep for at least six months.

SHROOM STEAK

PREP TIME: 130 MINUTES (INCLUDING RESTING) • COOK TIME: 25 MINUTES

THERE ARE MANY KINDS OF MUSHROOMS IN THE MUSHROOM KINGDOM, SUCH AS 1-UP MUSHROOMS, 3-UP MUSHROOMS, MINI MUSHROOMS, MEGA MUSHROOMS, AND SUPER MUSHROOMS, AND ALL OF THEM GRANT MARIO CERTAIN BENEFITS. IN THE *PAPER MARIO* SERIES, IT'S EVEN POSSIBLE TO USE VERY SPECIFIC MUSHROOMS AND OTHER ITEMS TO SERVE UP A SHROOM STEAK THAT REGENERATES A LOT MORE HEART POINTS THAN USUAL. OUR RECREATION OF THIS ICONIC DISH IS NOT ONLY A TRUE DELIGHT, IT'S A TRIBUTE TO THE MANY MUSHROOMS THAT EMPOWER OUR MARIO ADVENTURES.

★ ★ ★

TO MAKE THE STEAKS:

1. One hour before preparation, take the steaks out of the refrigerator, rub all over with oil, and allow to rest at room temperature.

2. Preheat the oven to 175°F.

3. On your stove, heat the oil in a heavy-bottomed, nonstick frying pan over high heat. As soon as the oil is hot, carefully place the steaks in the pan and sear, then flip and sear for another 10 seconds. Repeat until a nice crisp crust has formed on the meat and the meat feels noticeably firmer. (Five to six turns is generally enough.)

4. Insert an instant-read thermometer into the steak near the end of its cooking time to cook the steak to your desired level of doneness (125°F for rare, 135°F for medium-rare, 145°F for medium, 155°F for medium-well, or 165°F for well done). Turn the heat off, add the butter to the pan, season the meat to taste on both sides with sea salt and coarse ground pepper, and dredge the meat briefly through the melted butter. Transfer the steaks to a plate and "tent" the steaks with foil to rest while you prepare the sauce.

TO MAKE THE SHROOM SAUCE:

5. Add the shallots to the pan you just used for the steak and place over medium heat. Sweat for 2 to 3 minutes, until soft. Add the pancetta and sear. Add the mushrooms to the pan, season with the thyme, salt, and pepper to taste, and braise for 5 minutes. Then deglaze the pan with the wine and stock and reduce for 3 minutes.

6. As soon as the sauce has reduced a bit, sprinkle the flour over the pan and cook briefly. Stirring constantly, add the heavy cream and bring to a brief boil.

7. Add the meat drippings that have collected in the plate to the pan. Stir, then season to taste again with salt and pepper. Plate each steak, add a generous amount of mushroom sauce, then serve sprinkled with the scallion, coarse ground black pepper, and more salt, if you'd like.

MAKES 2 SERVINGS

STEAKS

2 steaks, ideally boneless rib eye (about 1½ inches thick)

1 tablespoon neutral-flavored oil, plus more to rub into the steaks

1 teaspoon butter

Coarse sea salt

Coarse ground black pepper

SHROOM SAUCE

1 shallot, diced

⅛ cup pancetta, diced

3.5 ounces mixed mushrooms, sliced

1 teaspoon dried thyme

Salt

Ground black pepper

5 teaspoons dry white wine

5 teaspoons beef stock

1½ teaspoons flour

5 teaspoons heavy cream

1 scallion, green part only, thinly sliced

MONA PIZZA'S ME6APIZZA

PREP TIME: 10 MINUTES • COOK TIME: 30 MINUTES

MARIO AND LUIGI ARE ITALIAN, SO IT'S NO SURPRISE THEY LIKE PIZZA! AND THE VERY BEST PIES IN THE WHOLE MUSHROOM KINGDOM ARE MADE AT MONA PIZZA IN DIAMOND CITY—NOT TO BE CONFUSED WITH PIZZA DINOSAUR, WHICH HAS THE WORST PIZZA! AND NO WONDER: PIZZA DINOSAUR IS ALL ABOUT MASS PRODUCTION WHEN IT COMES TO SUPPLYING THEIR 6,000 STORES. MONA PIZZA, FOR ITS PART, MAKES EVERYTHING BY HAND—JUST LIKE THIS HEARTY DELIGHT. BUT YOU WON'T FIND IT ON THE MENU AT MONA PIZZA. THIS EXCLUSIVE RECIPE IS FOUND NOWHERE ELSE BUT RIGHT HERE!

★ ★ ★

1. Preheat the oven to 400°F. Line a baking sheet with parchment paper.

2. Heat the olive oil in a frying pan over medium heat. Add the onion and garlic and sweat until translucent. Add the ground meat and cook on all sides, 3 to 4 minutes, until the meat is cooked through and nicely browned. Add the diced tomatoes, bring to a brief boil, then reduce the heat to low and simmer, uncovered, for 5 minutes, stirring frequently. Add the vinegar, season to taste with salt and pepper, and add 1 tablespoon of the Italian seasoning. Remove the tomato sauce from the heat and set aside.

3. Roll out the pizza dough on the counter to form a rectangle that fits on your baking sheet. Set the dough on the baking sheet.

4. Tear the drained mozzarella into bite-size pieces.

5. Spread the tomato sauce evenly over the pizza dough and top as desired with the ham, pepperoni, pineapple, and yellow chile. Sprinkle generously with the torn mozzarella and the remaining 1 tablespoon of Italian seasoning.

6. Bake for 13 to 15 minutes, depending on how crispy you like your crust. Remove from oven and sprinkle with fresh basil. Serve right away.

MAKES 6–8 SERVINGS

1 tablespoon olive oil

1 red onion, diced

1 garlic clove, minced

9 ounces ground beef and pork blend

9 ounces canned diced tomatoes

Dash balsamic vinegar

Salt

Ground black pepper

2 tablespoons Italian seasoning, divided

18 ounces ready-made pizza dough

7 ounces ham, diced

5 ounces pepperoni

5 ounces canned pineapple chunks, drained

1 small yellow chile, thinly sliced into rings

5 ounces fresh mozzarella, drained

Fresh basil leaves, for topping

TIP How you top your pizza is ultimately a personal choice. Just make sure you use the sauce as a base and don't be too stingy with the cheese. The rest is up to you!

DREAMY PASTA AND MEATBALLS

DIFFICULTY: 🍄🍄

PREP TIME: 10 MINUTES • COOK TIME: 50 MINUTES

WHEN IT COMES TO FOOD, PASTA IS HIGH ON MARIO AND LUIGI'S LIST. IN FACT, MARIO LOVES PASTA IN ALL ITS VARIETIES SO MUCH THAT WHEN HE GOES TO SLEEP IN *SUPER MARIO ODYSSEY* (2017), HE DREAMS OF A PROPER PASTA BINGE. BUT IT DOESN'T HAVE TO BE TOO FANCY FOR OUR FAVORITE PLUMBER. THIS COLORFUL, DREAMY PASTA OFFERS A TRADITIONAL TAKE, WITH HEARTY TOMATO SAUCE AND MEATBALLS. IT'S FANTASTICALLY DELICIOUS AND FIT FOR ANY REVERIE!

★ ★ ★

1. Combine the pork, parsley, sour cream, and nutmeg in a large bowl. Season to taste with salt and pepper. Shape the meat mixture into bite-size balls.

2. Heat the olive oil in a medium pot over medium heat. Add the shallot and garlic and sweat for a few minutes, until the shallot is translucent and the garlic is fragrant. Add the pancetta and brown. Add the celery and carrot and cook everything together for 2 minutes. Stir in the tomato paste and sauté briefly, then deglaze the pot with the stock and reduce for a bit.

3. Add the diced tomatoes and stir. Season with the celery salt, Italian seasoning, and sugar and simmer over low heat, stirring frequently, for 15 minutes. Then add the meatballs and simmer for another 20 minutes.

4. Meanwhile, cook the multicolored pasta in a large pot of generously salted water according to the instructions on the package. Drain the cooked pasta carefully and transfer to four bowls or deep plates. Top each serving with sauce and meatballs, sprinkle with Parmesan (if using), and serve garnished with a bit of fresh basil. Buon appetito!

MAKES 4 SERVINGS

18 ounces ground pork

½ bunch parsley, minced

2 tablespoons sour cream

Pinch freshly ground nutmeg

Salt

Ground black pepper

1 tablespoon olive oil

1 large shallot, minced

2 garlic cloves, minced

3.5 ounces pancetta, diced

1 rib celery, finely diced

1 carrot, diced

2 tablespoons tomato paste

3.5 fluid ounces vegetable stock

14 ounces canned diced tomatoes

Pinch celery salt

2 tablespoons Italian seasoning

Pinch sugar

9 ounces multicolored rotini or other spiral-shaped pasta

1.75 ounces Parmesan, freshly grated (optional)

Fresh basil, for garnish

KOOPASTA

PREP TIME: 5 MINUTES • COOK TIME: 10 MINUTES

THE MUSHROOM KINGDOM IS HOME TO MANY COOKS TO WHOM WE OWE MANY TASTY—AND A FEW DECIDEDLY UNAPPETIZING—DISHES. BUT ONLY TWO OF THEM ARE KNOWN FOR BEING ABLE TO MAKE THIS LEGENDARY DISH FROM *PAPER MARIO: THE THOUSAND-YEAR DOOR* (2004) JUST RIGHT: ZESS T. AND TAYCE T. NOW YOU CAN MAKE THIS DELIGHTFUL DISH YOURSELF!

★ ★ ★

1. Cook the pasta according to the package instructions in a large pot of generously salted water until it is al dente, about 5 to 7 minutes. Drain the cooked pasta through a strainer and return to the pot.

2. Meanwhile, purée the basil, Parmesan, pine nuts, garlic, and olive oil in a food processor. Alternatively, purée using an immersion blender for 3 minutes. If the pesto is too thick, add a bit more olive oil. Season to taste with salt and pepper.

3. Add the pesto to the pasta and stir until it is thoroughly coated. Divide among four bowls or soup plates, sprinkle with more Parmesan to taste, and arrange a lettuce leaf halfway over each serving as the "Koopa shell."

4. Serve immediately.

MAKES 4 SERVINGS

18 ounces green pasta (colored with spinach or Swiss chard, for example)

1 bunch fresh basil

1 ounce Parmesan freshly grated, plus more for garnish

1 ounce toasted pine nuts

1 garlic clove, minced

Dash olive oil, or as needed

Salt

Ground black pepper

4 nicely shaped lettuce leaves, to use as "shells"

DAISY'S CHEESY CHICKEN ENCHILADAS

PREP TIME: 20 MINUTES • COOK TIME: 30 MINUTES

PRINCESS DAISY, THE RULER OF SARASALAND, IS A SUPER ATHLETE. WHETHER SHE'S DRIVING A KART, SWINGING A GOLF CLUB, OR PLAYING TENNIS, SHE'S ALWAYS A STAR IN WHATEVER SHE DOES! BUT TOP ATHLETIC PERFORMANCE REQUIRES A LOT OF ENERGY, AND THAT'S JUST WHAT THIS DISH DELIVERS—PLUS, THE COMBINATION OF SAVORY CHEESE AND DELICATE FLOWERS IS A PERFECT MATCH FOR DAISY'S CHARMING BUT VOLATILE TEMPERAMENT. AFTER ALL, UNLIKE HER EVER-SYMPATHETIC FRIEND PEACH, DAISY WILL DO ANYTHING TO WIN. GOOD THING THESE ENCHILADAS ARE A CLEAR WINNER!

★ ★ ★

1. Heat the olive oil in a large frying pan over medium heat. Add the shallot and garlic and sweat until translucent. Add the chicken strips and lightly brown on all sides, about 6 to 8 minutes. Season to taste with salt and pepper, then add the paprika and chili powder. Remove from the heat.

2. Preheat the oven to 350°F on the convection setting, if you have it. Lightly brush an 8-by-12-inch casserole dish or baking pan with olive oil.

3. Spread the tortillas, one at a time, on the counter and brush the top side generously with the enchilada sauce. Top as desired with the kidney beans, green chiles, tomato, and cucumber. Place a serving of browned chicken in a horizontal line in the center of each tortilla. Sprinkle with the cheese and carefully roll together from the bottom side, making sure not to roll too tightly. Set the tortillas next to each other in the pan.

4. Pour the remaining sauce over the tortillas, then sprinkle with the remaining cheese. Bake for 20 to 30 minutes, depending on how brown you want the cheese and tortillas. Remove from the oven and allow to cool briefly.

5. Sprinkle with the cilantro immediately before serving. Garnish with edible flowers (if using) to give this dish more of a Daisy-like touch.

MAKES 6 ENCHILADAS

5 teaspoons olive oil, plus more for the pan

1 shallot, minced

1 garlic clove, minced

14 ounces chicken breast, cut into bite-size strips

Salt

Ground black pepper

Pinch smoked paprika

Pinch chili powder

6 large corn or flour tortillas

13.5 ounces canned red enchilada sauce

9 ounces canned kidney beans, drained

2 small green chiles

2 tomatoes, diced

½ cucumber, diced

9 ounces shredded cheese of your choice

5 sprigs fresh cilantro or parsley, chopped

Edible flowers, for topping (optional)

ALSO REQUIRED

8-by-12-inch casserole dish or baking pan

TIP Aside from kidney beans, onion, and garlic, these enchiladas can also be prepared with other or additional sautéed vegetables, such as corn. Pork, beef, and shrimp are also good alternatives to the chicken. Feel free to give your creativity free rein here, just like Daisy lets loose with all kinds of physical activity!

MISTAKE

PREP TIME: 20 MINUTES • COOK TIME: 50 MINUTES

WHAT DO YOU GET WHEN YOU GIVE ONE OF THE COOKS IN THE *PAPER MARIO* GAMES THE WRONG INGREDIENTS FOR A CERTAIN RECIPE OR DON'T FOLLOW THE RIGHT AMOUNTS? THAT'S RIGHT, A MISTAKE! WHEN IT COMES TO THIS DISH, THE MISTAKE IS INTENTIONAL—AND DOWNRIGHT DELICIOUS! YOU CAN EVEN EAT THE FISH BONES WITH NO PROBLEM. HEFF T. WOULD SURE LOVE IT, AT ANY RATE! THOUGH HE DOES EAT ANYTHING . . .

★ ★ ★

TO MAKE THE PARMESAN SKELETON:

1. Transfer the oats to a small bowl and cover with the boiling water. Stir briefly and allow to stand undisturbed for 10 minutes to absorb the water.

2. Meanwhile, preheat the oven to 300°F. Line a baking sheet with parchment paper.

3. Once the oats have expanded, add the Parmesan, egg white, salt, and pepper and knead together with your hands to form a very sticky but crumbly dough. Use most of the dough to shape a rope that is about ½ inch in diameter and about 8 inches long. Set it on the prepared baking sheet.

4. To make the "fish head," shape some of the leftover dough into a ball about the size of a golf ball and carefully press it flat. Set it on the counter and use a small, sharp knife to cut out a mouth and press an eye into the head.

5. Shape the fin and individual bones out of the remaining dough and press them into place along the "backbone" to form a fish skeleton (see image). In the process, make sure all the other elements are about the same thickness as the backbone so the Parmesan skeleton will bake evenly.

6. Bake for 25 to 30 minutes on the middle rack, then remove from the oven and leave on the baking sheet to cool completely. Carefully remove the skeleton from the paper. Watch out, it's fragile!

TO MAKE THE SPINACH RICE:

7. Put the rice in a strainer and rinse in cold running water until the runoff no longer looks cloudy. Then combine the rice, a generous pinch of salt, and the water in a medium pot over medium heat. Bring to a boil, immediately adjust

MAKES 3 SERVINGS

PARMESAN SKELETON

2¼ cups quick oats

1¾ cups boiling water

3.5 ounces grated Parmesan

1 egg white

½ teaspoon salt

Pinch ground black pepper

SPINACH RICE

1 cup basmati rice

Salt

1½ cups water

Zest of ½ lemon

4 tablespoons olive oil

1 onion, diced

2 garlic cloves, minced

18 ounces fresh baby spinach, coarsely chopped

Ground black pepper

VEGETABLE CURRY

One 13.5-ounce can coconut milk (unshaken)

2 tablespoons yellow curry paste

1 onion, diced

1 garlic clove, minced

1 carrot, peeled and diced

½ red bell pepper, diced

2 tablespoons raisins

Juice of ½ lime

1 to 2 tablespoons light soy sauce

Continued on page 58

Continued from page 57

the heat to low, cover, and cook for 12 to 15 minutes, or until all the water has been absorbed. Do not stir.

8. Meanwhile, heat the oil in a frying pan over medium heat. Add the onion and garlic and sweat until translucent. Add the spinach and combine. Once the spinach starts to wilt, add the cooked rice and lemon zest. Stir thoroughly to combine and season to taste with salt and pepper. Cook for 2 more minutes, then remove from the heat and keep warm until used.

TO MAKE THE VEGETABLE CURRY:

9. Open the can of coconut milk and skim the cream off (this is the solid mass that has formed on top of the coconut milk). Transfer it to a large frying pan, then add the curry paste, combining thoroughly. Bring to a boil over medium heat, then adjust the heat to maintain a simmer until small, oily bubbles form.

10. Add the onion and garlic and sweat for 5 minutes. Then add the carrot, bell pepper, and raisins, stir to combine, and sauté on all sides, stirring frequently. Pour in about 7 ounces of coconut milk (about half of the can; reserve the rest for another use) and bring to a brief boil. Then adjust the heat to low and simmer for 5 minutes. Season to taste with a bit of lime juice and light soy sauce and reduce, stirring occasionally, until very little liquid is left.

11. Finally, arrange the spinach rice, vegetable curry, and Parmesan skeleton on a serving plate and serve immediately.

ROAST WHACKA BUMP

PREP TIME: 10 MINUTES • COOK TIME: 140 TO 160 MINUTES (INCLUDING BRAISING)

WHACKAS ARE CUTE BLUE MOLE-LIKE CREATURES THAT DROP A VERY USEFUL ITEM, WHACKA BUMP, WHEN THEY ARE WHACKED OR JUMPED ON. WHACKA BUMPS ARE SO HIGHLY PRIZED, IN FACT, THAT THE WHACKAS ARE NOW OFFICIALLY AN ENDANGERED SPECIES. BUT DON'T WORRY, NO WHACKAS ARE HARMED IN THE MAKING OF THIS JUICY SUNDAY ROAST!

★ ★ ★

TO MAKE THE ROAST:

1. Preheat the oven to 425°F.

2. Vigorously rub the roast all over with salt. Then set it, rind side down, in a Dutch oven and pour warm water over it until the rind is fully covered, but not the meat. Roast, uncovered, for 25 minutes to precook the rind. Then transfer the roast to a carving board and use a large, sharp knife to cut a crosshatch pattern into the rind. Place a whole clove at each intersection.

3. Rinse and dry the Dutch oven, then set it over medium heat. Warm the olive oil in it, then add the roast with the clove-studded rind facing up. Add the onions, celery root, carrots, and leek. Sauté until the vegetables are lightly browned, about 5 to 6 minutes. Add the garlic, peppercorns, bay leaf, and hot water.

4. Meanwhile, adjust the oven temperature to 400°F.

5. Set the Dutch oven, uncovered, inside the oven and cook for 1 hour and 30 minutes to 2 hours, or until the meat is done and very tender. During cooking, make sure to refill the evaporating water regularly with the stock. Shortly before the end of the cooking time, combine 1 tablespoon of salt and a bit of water in a cup and brush the rind with it several times so it gets nice and crisp.

MAKES 5–6 SERVINGS

ROAST

2.2 pounds pork roast

Salt

10 whole cloves

1 tablespoon olive oil

2 onions, diced

1 knob celery root (celeriac), diced

2 carrots, diced

1 leek, thinly sliced into rings

2 garlic cloves, minced

10 whole black peppercorns

1 bay leaf

2 cups hot water

17 fluid ounces beef stock

4½ teaspoons cornstarch

Ground black pepper

POTATO WEDGES

1.75 pounds russet or similar potatoes

2 tablespoons sunflower oil

2 tablespoons olive oil

1 teaspoon fine salt

1 teaspoon paprika

½ teaspoon ground black pepper

1 teaspoon coarse sea salt

STEAMED CARROTS

¼ cup (½ stick) butter

1 bunch baby carrots, peeled and tops removed

2 pinches salt

2 pinches sugar

1 tablespoon water

Minced fresh parsley, for topping

ALSO REQUIRED

Dutch oven

Continued on page 60

Continued from page 59

6. Remove the roast from the Dutch oven and allow to rest briefly (covered loosely with aluminum foil) on a carving board. Strain the vegetables over a clean pot to catch the juices. Heat the liquid over medium heat and maintain a simmer. Meanwhile, combine the cornstarch and a bit of cold water. Gradually stir the cornstarch slurry into the simmering juices until the sauce is nice and thick, then season to taste with salt and pepper.

TO MAKE THE POTATO WEDGES:

7. Wash the potatoes thoroughly, drain, and slice lengthwise into sixths or eighths, leaving the peel on.

8. Preheat the oven to 400°F on the convection setting, if you have it (or 425°F on the normal setting). Line a baking sheet with parchment paper.

9. Combine sunflower oil, olive oil, fine salt, and paprika in a large bowl. Stir in the pepper, add the potato wedges, and combine so the potatoes are coated all over with the oil and seasonings.

10. Set the wedges individually on the parchment paper, leaving a bit of space between them, and bake for about 30 minutes, until crisp and golden. Turn halfway through so the potatoes are nice and crisp on both sides. Sprinkle with the coarse salt before serving.

TO MAKE THE STEAMED CARROTS:

11. Melt the butter in a small pot over medium heat. Once the butter begins to brown, add the whole baby carrots. Season with the salt and sugar and add the water. Adjust the heat to low, cover, and steam for about 8 minutes, or until the carrots are tender (but not too tender). Shake the pot once during cooking, without taking off the lid. Sprinkle with the parsley.

12. Carve the roast into finger-thick slices and serve together with the potato wedges, baby carrots, and sauce.

TIP This roast is also excellent served with Whacka Bumps (see page 120).

SHROOM FRY

PREP TIME: 10 MINUTES • COOK TIME: 25 MINUTES

MANY KINDS OF MUSHROOMS ARE FOUND ALL AROUND THE MARIO UNIVERSE, EACH WITH A DIFFERENT EFFECT. WHILE A SUPER MUSHROOM MAKES MARIO BIGGER AND BETTER ABLE TO WITHSTAND ENEMY ATTACKS, A PROPELLER MUSHROOM GIVES HIM THE POWER TO FLY. THE MUSHROOMS IN THIS DISH HAVE A VERY SPECIAL EFFECT, TOO: THEY MAKE YOU HUNGRY FOR MORE! BE SURE TO MAKE ENOUGH SHROOM FRY FOR EVERYONE—ESPECIALLY YOURSELF!

★ ★ ★

1. Rinse the mushrooms, pat dry with paper towels, and cut into bite-size pieces.

2. Melt the butter in a large frying pan over medium heat. Add the pancetta and brown on all sides (2 to 3 minutes). Add the shallots and sweat until translucent (2 to 3 minutes). Add the mushrooms and thyme, stir well to combine, and sauté on all sides for several minutes, until the mushrooms begin to shrivel and release their liquid.

3. Deglaze the pan with the stock and port wine (if using), adjust the heat to low, and add the heavy cream. Add the chile and reduce for 10 minutes. Then season to taste with salt, pepper, and sugar and sprinkle with chives to serve.

MAKES ABOUT 4 SERVINGS

18 ounces mixed mushrooms (such as button mushrooms, chanterelles, porcini mushrooms)

1 tablespoon butter

7 ounces pancetta, diced

2 shallots, minced

1 tablespoon dried thyme

3.5 fluid ounces vegetable or wild mushroom stock

Scant ¼ cup port wine (optional)

2 tablespoons heavy cream

1 small red chile, thinly sliced into rings

Salt

Ground black pepper

Pinch sugar

½ bunch fresh chives, chopped

STUPENDOUS STEW

PREP TIME: 10 MINUTES • COOK TIME: 40 MINUTES

THE LUNCHEON KINGDOM IS THE HOME OF THE VOLBONANS, WHO ARE KNOWN FOR THEIR STUPENDOUS STEW, WHICH THEY COOK ON MOUNT VOLBONO. IN *SUPER MARIO ODYSSEY* (2017), BOWSER TAKES BOTH PRINCESS PEACH AND THE TASTY STEW, INTENDING TO SERVE IT AT THE RECEPTION AFTER HE MARRIES HER! MARIO MUST TRAVERSE THE LUNCHEON KINGDOM TO SPOIL HIS ARCHENEMY'S PARTY, RESCUE HIS LOVE, AND SAVE THE STEW. AND IT'S WORTH THE EFFORT—ONE BITE, AND YOU'LL SEE WHY THIS STEW HAS SUCH A LEGENDARY REPUTATION.

★ ★ ★

1. Melt the butter in a medium pot over medium heat. Add the flour and whisk swiftly for 2 minutes, until the roux is golden brown. Then, working in several batches, gradually add the stock, stirring until all of the liquid has been absorbed after each addition. Continue until you have used up all the stock and there are no longer any visible lumps of flour.

2. Stir in the heavy cream, bring to a brief boil, then adjust the heat to maintain a simmer for 5 minutes, or until thickened slightly.

3. Add the chicken, carrots, mushrooms, bell peppers, and peas to the pot and simmer for 15 to 20 minutes, stirring frequently. Once the meat is done, season to taste with salt, pepper, lemon juice, and Worcestershire sauce.

4. Serve with cooked rice.

MAKES 4 SERVINGS

3 tablespoons butter

3 tablespoons flour

24 fluid ounces chicken or poultry stock

¾ cup plus 2 tablespoons heavy cream

1.5 pounds boneless skinless chicken breast, coarsely cubed

11 ounces carrots, diced

9 ounces mushrooms, sliced

¼ red bell pepper, diced

¼ green bell pepper, diced

¼ yellow bell pepper, diced

5 ounces frozen peas

Salt

Ground black pepper

Dash lemon juice

Dash Worcestershire sauce

Cooked rice, for serving

DESSERTS

FRUIT PARFAIT

PREP TIME: 10 MINUTES • COOK TIME: 15 MINUTES

IN *PAPER MARIO: THE THOUSAND-YEAR DOOR* (2004), CHEF ZESS T. USES VARIOUS COMBINATIONS OF INGREDIENTS TO MAKE A FRUIT PARFAIT, SUCH AS PEACH AND MANGO, MANGO AND GRADUAL SYRUP, OR A PEACH AND A SERVING OF SPACE FOOD. AS FOR US, WE MAKE THIS REFRESHING, CREAMY PARFAIT OUT OF YOGURT, MASCARPONE CREAM, AND—YOU GUESSED IT—FRUIT!

⭐ ⭐ ⭐

TO MAKE THE FRUIT SAUCE:

1. Combine the frozen fruit and sugar in a small pot over medium-high heat. Bring to a boil, then reduce the heat to low and simmer for 10 minutes, breaking up and mashing the fruit with a spoon in the process. Remove from the heat, allow to cool briefly, and refrigerate until ready to assemble.

TO MAKE THE MASCARPONE CREAM:

2. Combine the heavy cream, sugar, and vanilla extract in a medium bowl and beat with an electric mixer until stiff peaks form (4 to 5 minutes).

3. Carefully combine the Greek yogurt and mascarpone in a separate bowl. Then fold in the whipped cream.

TO ASSEMBLE:

4. Layer the parfait into eight serving dishes by starting with a layer of mascarpone cream, then topping as desired with the granola, fresh berries, and fruit sauce. Repeat twice, or until the glasses are three-fourths full. Sprinkle with the granola and top with a few especially attractive berries.

5. Cover loosely with plastic wrap and refrigerate until served.

MAKES 8 SERVINGS

FRUIT SAUCE

9 ounces frozen fruit (such as mixed berries), thawed

¼ cup sugar

MASCARPONE CREAM

1 cup plus 5 teaspoons heavy cream

½ cup sugar

1 tablespoon vanilla extract

1 cup plus 5 teaspoons low-fat Greek yogurt

1 cup plus 5 teaspoons mascarpone

ASSEMBLY

14 ounces granola

2 pounds fresh mixed berries (such as blueberries, raspberries, blackberries), washed and patted dry

ALSO REQUIRED

8 serving dishes

THE DOUBLE-CROSSERS

PREP TIME: 20 MINUTES • COOK TIME: 30 MINUTES

THIS DELECTABLE LEMON BLACKBERRY MOUSSE IS INSPIRED BY *MARIO PARTY 8* (2007), WHERE WARIO AND WALUIGI FIGHT FUN AND ENTERTAINING DUELS AS A TEAM UNDER THE NAME DOUBLE-CROSSERS. THIS DESSERT TAKES ITS COLOR SCHEME FROM THE CHARACTERS' QUIRKY LOOK. WHEN IT COMES TO TASTE, THOUGH, IT'S QUITE A BIT SWEETER THAN THESE GUYS!

★ ★ ★

1. Combine the white chocolate, milk, and powdered sugar in a small pot over medium heat and whisk until the chocolate has melted and the sugar has dissolved completely. Then remove from the heat and allow to cool.

2. Place the yogurt in a bowl, add the yellow food coloring, and whisk briefly. Stir in the cooled milk mixture, cover with plastic wrap, and refrigerate for about 15 minutes.

3. Meanwhile, use an electric mixer to beat the heavy cream in a bowl until stiff peaks form. Once the yogurt mixture has cooled completely, fold it in.

4. Set aside a few especially appealing blackberries to use as garnish. Combine the remaining blackberries and sugar in a suitable pot over high heat, stirring constantly, until the mixture comes to a boil. Then reduce the heat to low and simmer for 20 to 25 minutes, or until the fruit reduction is nice and smooth but still contains bits of fruit. Remove from the heat and allow to cool briefly.

5. Use a tablespoon to layer the yogurt mixture and fruit sauce into six serving glasses, alternating between them, until the glasses are three-fourths full. Garnish with the reserved blackberries and sprinkle with lemon zest to taste.

6. Cover with plastic wrap and refrigerate until served.

MAKES 6 SERVINGS

½ cup plus 1 tablespoon white chocolate chips

6 tablespoons milk

2 tablespoons powdered sugar

2 cups plus 3 tablespoons Greek yogurt

1 to 2 drops of yellow food coloring

¾ cup plus 2 tablespoons heavy cream

18 ounces frozen blackberries

⅓ cup plus 1 tablespoon turbinado or raw sugar

Lemon zest, for topping

ALSO REQUIRED

6 serving glasses

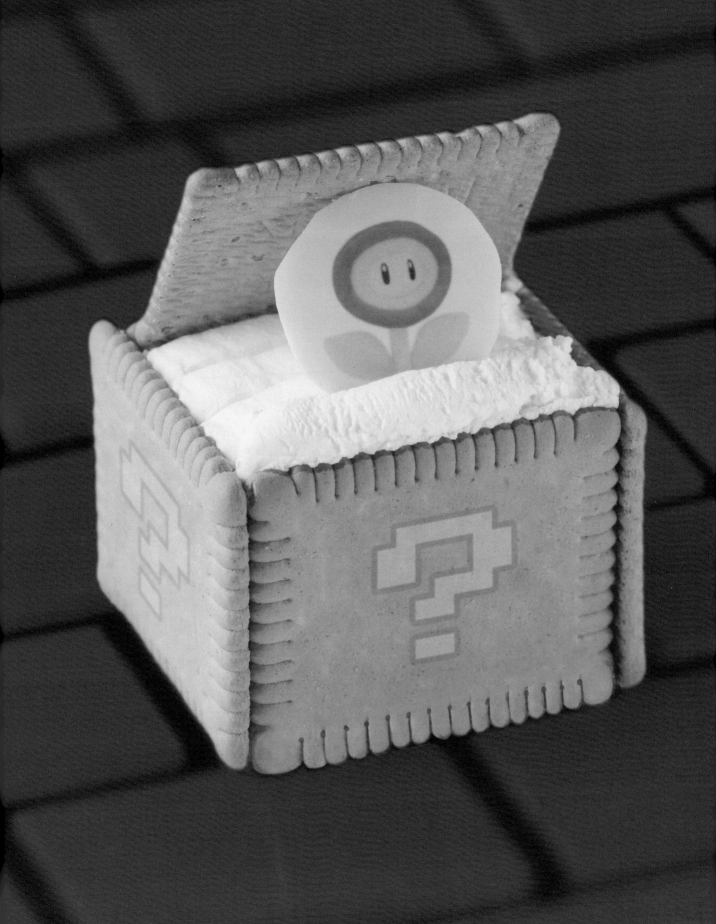

? BLOCK TIRAMISU

PREP TIME: 30 MINUTES • COOK TIME: 5 MINUTES

? BLOCKS OFFER A WEALTH OF SURPRISES IN THE MARIO UNIVERSE. YOU NEVER KNOW WHAT YOU MIGHT GET IF YOU JUMP INTO ONE OR HIT IT. SOMETIMES IT'S COINS, SOMETIMES IT'S A SUPER MUSHROOM, FIRE FLOWER, OR OTHER USEFUL ITEM. WITH THIS ? BLOCK, THOUGH, YOU KNOW FROM THE START WHAT TO EXPECT INSIDE: DELICIOUS, CREAMY TIRAMISU! AND YOU DON'T EVEN HAVE TO RISK A CONCUSSION OR A BROKEN ANKLE BY SMASHING YOUR HEAD OR FEET AGAINST BLOCKS TO ENJOY THIS REFINED DESSERT. YOU JUST HAVE TO WALK INTO YOUR KITCHEN!

★ ★ ★

1. Melt the white chocolate in a double boiler or bain-marie or by heating in 10-second intervals in the microwave. Stir until the chocolate has melted completely and is nice and smooth.

2. Place 12 of the butter cookies on the counter. For each ? Block, carefully dip four additional cookies in the melted chocolate on one side and place them on the bottom cookie to form a small box (see image). Use the chocolate as "glue" to stick the cookies together. You can also use toothpicks to hold them in place until the structure has set and stands on its own. At the end of this step, you should have 12 ? Blocks, open at the top. Allow to cool completely.

3. Meanwhile, combine the powdered sugar, vanilla extract, mascarpone, and yogurt in a bowl and carefully combine with an electric mixer.

4. Use the mixer to beat the heavy cream in a separate bowl until stiff peaks form. Then carefully fold the whipped cream into the mascarpone mixture with a spoon.

5. Cut the ladyfingers down the middle so one piece fits into each box.

6. Transfer a generous tablespoon of the cream into each box, place a piece of ladyfinger on top, and cover with another spoon of cream. Smooth the top of the cream. Place a butter cookie as a lid on the "back" of the ? Block, using chocolate to hold it in place as necessary. (You may need to reheat the chocolate briefly in the microwave to make it liquid again.)

7. Garnish each ? Block Tiramisu with a Mario chocolate cupcake topper and refrigerate for at least 1 hour before serving.

8. Enjoy promptly.

MAKES 12 SERVINGS

7 ounces white chocolate, coarsely chopped

72 rectangular butter cookies

1 cup powdered sugar

2 tablespoons vanilla extract

2 cups plus 3 tablespoons mascarpone

1⅓ cups Greek yogurt

1⅓ cups heavy cream

6 ladyfingers

12 store-bought Mario chocolate cupcake toppers

TIP If you want to really put the finishing touch on your ? Blocks to give them that special Mario look, you can use the rest of the chocolate and a dark-colored edible marker to give the cookie sides of each box the typical question mark.

WING CAP DREAM

PREP TIME: 10 MINUTES (PLUS 3 HOURS FOR CHILLING)
COOK TIME: 15 TO 25 MINUTES (PLUS 1 HOUR TO SET COMPLETELY)

THE WING CAP WAS MARIO'S SIGNATURE POWER-UP IN *SUPER MARIO 64* (1996), ALLOWING HIM TO SOAR THROUGH THE OPEN SKIES. MARIO IS NO STRANGER TO LIMITLESS HORIZONS—WHETHER HE'S TAKING THE RAINBOW RIDE, RIDING ON THE SAND BIRD, EXPLORING THE FLUFFY BLUFF GALAXY, OR EVEN FACING BOWSER AMONG FOREBODING PURPLE-AND-PINK CLOUDS, HE HAS BEEN TOUCHING THE SKY FOR DECADES NOW. BUT IT WAS THE WING CAP THAT ALLOWED MARIO TO SOAR AROUND IN A 3D SKY FOR THE FIRST TIME, AND SO IT'S THE WING CAP WE'VE NAMED THIS DESSERT AFTER. MADE FROM LUSCIOUS BLUE GELATIN AND WHITE WHIPPED CREAM CLOUDS, THE WING CAP DREAM WILL MAKE YOU WANT TO GRAB *YOUR* CAP AND GLIDE AMONG THE CLOUDS!

★ ★ ★

1. Combine the heavy cream and sour cream in a medium bowl and beat with an electric mixer until the mixture has thickened noticeably. Add the powdered sugar and lemon juice and continue beating until stiff peaks form. Cover with plastic wrap and refrigerate for 3 hours. Stir again to combine before using.

2. Fill a pastry bag with the cream and squeeze cloud shapes (see image) onto the insides of six tall glasses. Proceed gradually, allowing the cream to dry before turning the glass a bit to create the next clouds. Continue in this way, decorating all of the glasses with clouds of cream.

3. Meanwhile, prepare the gelatin dessert according to the instructions on the package. In most cases, this involves bringing 2¼ cups of water to a boil in a pot. Then add the powder, adjust the heat to low, and continue stirring until the powder has dissolved completely.

4. Transfer the mixture to a bowl and refrigerate for about 10 to 20 minutes so that it sets but not so much that it doesn't flow!

5. Carefully pour the cooled gelatin through a funnel into the prepared glasses. Gradually fill the glasses almost to the brim, then chill for at least 1 hour. Refrigerate until consumed.

MAKES 6 SERVINGS

1 cup plus 5 teaspoons heavy cream, cold

2 tablespoons sour cream, cold

2 tablespoons powdered sugar

1 tablespoon lemon juice

10.5 ounces blue gelatin dessert powder

ALSO REQUIRED

Pastry bag

6 tall serving glasses

Funnel

FRUIT BOMBS

PREP TIME: 10 MINUTES • COOK TIME: 5 MINUTES

DONKEY KONG COUNTRY: TROPICAL FREEZE (2014) FEATURES WATERMELON FUSE BOMBS, WHICH CAN BE THROWN TO CLEAR A PATH, REVEAL A SECRET BONUS ROOM, OR DO SOME SERIOUS DAMAGE. THESE FRUIT BOMBS, FOR THEIR PART, ARE MUCH LESS DESTRUCTIVE—AND MUCH TASTIER, THANKS TO A VARIETY OF FRUITS FOUND ON DONKEY KONG'S ISLAND: KIWI, BERRIES, BANANAS, PLUS ENOUGH DELICIOUS CREAMY PUDDING TO CALM EVEN THE ANGRIEST GORILLA!

★ ★ ★

TO MAKE THE SAUCE:

1. Put the gelatin powder, cornstarch, and sugar in a small saucepan and mix. Add the water and mix well. Bring to a brief boil over medium-high heat, until the mixture bubbles and turns clear, then remove from the heat.

TO MAKE THE VANILLA PUDDING:

2. Meanwhile, in a medium bowl, combine the pudding mix, sugar, and ¼ cup of the milk until there are no more lumps.

3. Transfer the remaining 1¾ cups of milk to a small pot and bring to a boil over medium heat, stirring constantly. Whisk in the pudding mixture and simmer, stirring constantly, for about 1 minute, or until the pudding has thickened noticeably. Remove from the heat.

TO ASSEMBLE:

4. Evenly fill the tartlet shells to the brim with the still-hot pudding. Smooth the tops. Then spoon the sauce over the tartlets and allow to cool briefly. Garnish as desired with fruit, then serve promptly.

MAKES 12 FRUIT BOMBS

SAUCE

½ tablespoon unflavored gelatin powder

4 tablespoons cornstarch

1 tablespoon sugar

1 cup lukewarm water

VANILLA PUDDING

1 package vanilla pudding mix

3 tablespoons plus 1 teaspoon sugar

2 cups milk, divided

ASSEMBLY

12 ready-made tartlet shells

11 ounces fresh fruit of your choice, peeled and cut as necessary to fit into tartlets

YOSHI'S FRUIT CRÊPES

PREP TIME: 35 MINUTES (INCLUDING COOLING) • COOK TIME: 20 MINUTES

YOSHIS LOVE FRUIT, AND WITH GOOD REASON! FRUIT IS BOTH TASTY AND HEALTHY. APPLES, BANANAS, PEACHES, MANGOES, AND MELONS—THESE CUTE LITTLE GUYS JUST CAN'T GET ENOUGH. AND WHO DOESN'T LOVE CRÊPES? SO WE PUT THEM TOGETHER AND WHIPPED UP SOME OF THESE DELECTABLE FRUIT CRÊPES IN TRIBUTE TO THE YOSHIS!

★ ★ ★

1. In a large bowl, combine the flour, milk, salt, and eggs and beat with an electric mixer until the flour has been fully absorbed and bubbles begin to form in the batter. Cover loosely with plastic wrap and refrigerate for 30 minutes.

2. Meanwhile, use the electric mixer to whip the heavy cream in a separate bowl until stiff peaks form. Refrigerate the whipped cream.

3. Wash the fruit and pat dry with paper towels. Cut into bite-size pieces, cover with plastic wrap, and set aside.

4. Add the mineral water to the chilled batter and roughly whisk.

5. Heat a large frying pan over high heat. Then adjust the heat to medium and add some butter to melt and coat the pan. To make each crêpe, add a ladleful of batter to the pan and gently swirl to distribute it evenly. Cook for 30 to 40 seconds on the first side, until lightly golden, then carefully turn it over with a pancake turner and repeat on the other side. Set on a plate and loosely cover with aluminum foil to keep the crêpe warm. Repeat this process until all the batter is used up.

6. To serve, place one crêpe each on a large plate and spread whipped cream over half of it. Sprinkle with fruit and drizzle with the fruit sauce as desired. Fold over to form a half-moon shape, dust with powdered sugar, and enjoy immediately.

MAKES 16 CRÊPES

4 cups plus 2 tablespoons flour

3⅓ cups milk

Pinch salt

3 large eggs

2 cups plus 3 tablespoons heavy cream

1.5 pounds mixed fresh fruit (such as apples, raspberries, bananas, blueberries)

2 tablespoons highly carbonated mineral water

Butter, for the pan

7 fluid ounces raspberry fruit sauce

Powdered sugar, for dusting

BANANA CHIPS

PREP TIME: 10 MINUTES • COOK TIME: ABOUT 8 HOURS

NOWADAYS, PEOPLE THINK OF BOWSER AS MARIO'S ARCHENEMY. BUT THE FIRST MEETING BETWEEN MARIO AND DONKEY KONG WAS ILL FATED, TOO. IN THE CLASSIC VERSION OF *DONKEY KONG* (1981), DONKEY KONG KIDNAPS PAULINE, NOW MAYOR OF NEW DONK CITY, WHICH STARTS EVERYONE'S FAVORITE PLUMBER ON HIS QUEST TO RESCUE HER. THERE WAS QUITE A BIT OF TENSION BETWEEN DONKEY KONG AND MARIO FOR A WHILE AFTER THAT, BUT NOW THEY'RE GOOD FRIENDS. IN FACT, THERE'S ONLY ONE THING DONKEY KONG LOVES MORE THAN HIS FRIENDS: BANANAS! OR, TO BE MORE SPECIFIC, BANANA CHIPS! THESE BANANA CHIPS!

★ ★ ★

1. Preheat the oven to 175°F on the convection setting, if you have it.

2. Peel the bananas and slice thinly and evenly, ideally ⅛ to less than ¼ inch thick. The thinner the slices, the crunchier the chips will be!

3. Line two baking sheets with parchment paper and spread the banana slices in a single layer across the sheet so the pieces do not touch.

4. Cut the lemon in half and juice it. Sprinkle a few drops of lemon juice over the banana slices so they do not turn brown. Use a light hand, or the chips will be sour!

5. Place the baking sheets on the second and fourth racks in the oven and insert the handle of a wooden spoon into the oven door so the door stays open a crack and the steam generated inside can escape. Allow to dry in the oven for 6 to 8 hours, turning the chips over halfway through the drying time. The banana chips are done when they are crunchy and golden. Then turn off the oven and allow the chips to stand and continue to dry for another 30 minutes with the oven door open.

6. Transfer the entire sheet of parchment paper onto a cooling rack and allow chips to cool completely. These chips will keep for three to four months in airtight sealed containers.

MAKES 8 TO 10 SERVINGS

20 bananas

1 lemon

 TIP It is best to use very ripe bananas for this recipe. Ideally, the bananas will have developed brown spots on the peel but still be firm enough to cut. This will bring out the fullest flavor in the chips.

DIFFICULTY:

BANANA'S BANANA SPLIT

PREP TIME: 10 MINUTES

"BANANA, SPLIT" IS A MINIGAME FROM *SUPER MARIO PARTY* (2018). THE NAME IS MEANT QUITE
LITERALLY: THE OBJECT OF THE GAME IS TO CORRECTLY ALIGN TWO HALVES OF A BANANA
AS QUICKLY AS POSSIBLE. WITH THIS DESSERT, HOWEVER, YOU'LL WANT TO SPLIT IT WITH A LOVED ONE!
THIS DELICACY OF ICE CREAM, BANANA, CHOCOLATE, AND CREAM, GARNISHED WITH
JUICY SUGARY CHERRIES, IS SIMPLY TOO DELICIOUS TO KEEP FOR YOURSELF.

★ ★ ★

1. Arrange four large scoops of ice cream in the center of an oblong shallow bowl or plate with a raised rim.

2. Peel the banana and cut in half vertically. Place one half on one side of the ice cream, and the other half on the other, following the long side of the dish.

3. Place one cocktail cherry on top of each ice cream scoop and garnish with whipped cream to taste.

4. Drizzle with some of the juice or syrup from the cocktail cherry jar and sprinkle with chocolate shavings.

5. Serve with two spoons and enjoy with your favorite person!

MAKES 2 SERVINGS

1 banana

4 scoops banana chocolate ice cream

4 cocktail cherries

Whipped cream, for topping

Juice or syrup from the cocktail cherries, for topping

Chocolate shavings, for topping

ALSO REQUIRED

Ice cream scoop

GOOMBA COCOA POPS

PREP TIME: 20 MINUTES • COOK TIME: 5 MINUTES

GOOMBAS ARE LITTLE BROWN CREATURES FROM THE MUSHROOM KINGDOM. IN THE GAMES, THEY WERE ORIGINALLY CONCEIVED AS A KIND OF COUNTERPOINT TO THE KOOPAS, SINCE THE DEVELOPERS THOUGHT IT WOULD BE BEST TO ADD SOME ENEMIES THAT WERE EASIER TO DEFEAT. IN MOST CASES, IT TAKES JUST ONE JUMP TO SEE THEM OFF. GOOMBA COCOA POPS ARE SIMILAR THAT WAY: JUST ONE TASTY BITE AND THEY'RE GONE!

★ ★ ★

1. Melt the chocolate in a double boiler or bain-marie, or by heating in 10-second intervals in the microwave, and stir until no lumps remain.

2. Combine the cereal and almonds in a large bowl and pour the melted chocolate over the mixture. Add the vanilla extract and stir carefully to combine.

3. Line two baking sheets with parchment paper and arrange 24 skewers evenly on the sheets, leaving room between them.

4. Use a tablespoon to drop a small amount of the mixture onto the top of each skewer, then press into place around the skewer with your fingers and allow to set at room temperature (about 10 to 15 minutes).

5. Enjoy immediately. Store leftover cocoa pops (if there are any!) in an airtight container.

MAKES 24 POPS

1 cup plus 3 tablespoons milk chocolate chips

10 ounces chocolate crisp rice cereal

1 cup chopped or slivered almonds

1 to 2 drops vanilla extract

ALSO REQUIRED

24 wooden skewers

BAKED GOODS

? BLOCK CAKE

PREP TIME: 60 MINUTES • COOK TIME: 20 MINUTES

DID YOU KNOW ? BLOCKS—THE SECOND MOST COMMON TYPE OF BLOCK IN THE MARIO UNIVERSE—HAVE A FAIRLY SAD BACKSTORY? THEY ARE ACTUALLY TOADS THAT WERE TRANSFORMED BY BOWSER! THIS CAKE THANKFULLY DOESN'T CONTAIN ENCHANTED TOADS. INSTEAD, IT'S MADE FROM A BUNCH OF DELICIOUS INGREDIENTS, ALL TOPPED WITH DELECTABLE BUTTERCREAM! SO THERE'S NO REASON TO BE SAD FOR THIS ? BLOCK!

★ ★ ★

TO MAKE THE CAKE:

1. Preheat the oven to 350°F. Line the baking pan with parchment paper.

2. In a large bowl, combine the eggs, sugar, and vanilla extract and beat with an electric mixer until creamy. Then add the flour, baking soda, and cream of tartar and combine.

3. Pour the batter into the the baking pan and smooth the top.

4. Bake for 20 minutes, or until a toothpick inserted into the middle comes out clean. Then remove from the oven, allow to cool to room temperature, and then remove the cake from the pan by inverting it onto a wire rack. Allow the cake to cool completely while you make the frosting.

TO MAKE THE FROSTING:

5. Use the electric mixer to beat the butter in a bowl until it has lightened considerably in color; gradually add the cream cheese and powdered sugar by tablespoons, mixing carefully to combine with each addition. Add the food coloring to produce a bright yellow color.

TO ASSEMBLE:

6. Cut the cake in half horizontally and then vertically, creating four cakes that are 4 inches by 4 inches. Stack three or four of the cakes to create a cube (depending on how much it rose), using a spoon to hollow out the middle piece or two of cake. Make sure to leave enough of the walls intact and thick enough that the cake has a solid structure. Coat each of the layers with a thin layer of frosting, fill the hollow with candy as desired, then neatly place the top piece of cake on top. Use the remaining frosting to roughly frost the cake on all sides.

7. Roll out the fondant and use a 1½-inch cookie cutter to cut out 20 circles. Using a small, sharp knife, cut out five question marks and five small rectangles. Decorate the top and four sides of the cake with the fondant (see image) and allow to dry briefly before serving.

MAKES 1 CAKE
(6 to 8 servings)

CAKE

4 eggs

1 cup sugar

1 tablespoon vanilla extract

2 cups flour

¾ teaspoon baking soda

1½ teaspoon cream of tartar

FROSTING

1 cup (2 sticks) plus 2 tablespoons butter, at room temperature

10.5 ounces cream cheese, at room temperature

1⅓ cups powdered sugar

Few drops yellow gel food coloring

ASSEMBLY

Candy and sweet decorations, such as M&M's, gummy candies, sprinkles, for filling

5.5 ounces white ready-rolled fondant

ALSO REQUIRED

Square baking pan (about 8 by 8 inches)

1½-inch round cookie cutters

TIP Don't be fooled by the size of the cake in the picture—this ? Block Cake is smaller than it looks here. So don't worry that the cake mix won't be enough!

PIRANHA PLANT CAKE POPS

PREP TIME: 60 MINUTES • COOK TIME: 5 MINUTES

MOST PIRANHA PLANTS, CARNIVOROUS FLORA WITH A PENCHANT FOR TAKING BIG CHOMPS OUT OF MARIO AND FRIENDS, STICK TO THEIR WARP PIPES OR STAY ROOTED WHERE THEY GROW. HOWEVER, SOME OF THEM, SUCH AS PETEY PIRANHA, CAN WALK AROUND ON THEIR OWN ROOTS! WE'VE FIRMLY PLANTED THESE DELICIOUS, CHOCOLATEY PIRANHA PLANT CAKE POPS IN CHARMING POTS SO THEY CAN'T CAUSE ANY TROUBLE. THEY'LL BE A RICH, NON-BITING ADDITION TO ANY GATHERING.

1. Place the heavy cream in a small pot over medium heat and bring to a brief boil. Remove from the heat and add the chocolate. Whisk until the chocolate has dissolved completely. Allow to cool.

2. Line a cutting board or other surface with parchment paper.

3. Crumble the first pound cake in a large bowl as finely as possible. Add the cooled chocolate mixture and stir to combine thoroughly. Scoop out by the tablespoon and use your hands to shape the mixture into 1-inch balls. Then set the balls on the prepared cutting board and refrigerate for about 30 minutes to cool and set. You should have about 40 balls.

4. Melt the sugar glaze, either using a double boiler or bain-marie, or by heating in 10-second intervals in the microwave. Dip a cake pop stick about ½ inch into the glaze and insert it into the middle of each cake pop so it holds firmly. Then refrigerate the cake pops for 15 minutes.

5. Use a small, sharp knife to carefully cut a mouth into each cake pop so it looks like a Piranha Plant (see image). Reheat the glaze so it is liquid again. Fully immerse each cake pop in the glaze, top down. Hold in place briefly for the excess glaze to drip off.

6. Coarsely crumble the chocolate cake so it looks like soil and fill the pots (if using) with it.

7. Insert the cake pops into the pots with the cake "soil." Allow to dry for several minutes. Use the white writing icing to draw on the mouth, teeth, and dots and allow to dry briefly again.

8. Finally, arrange a marzipan leaf to the left and right of the cake pop stick on top of the "soil." Line the pots up on a tray and serve.

MAKES 40 CAKE POPS

¾ cup plus 2 tablespoons heavy cream

1 cup plus 3 tablespoons milk chocolate, coarsely chopped

14 ounces pound cake of your choice

7 ounces red candy melts

14 ounces chocolate pound cake

1 small tube white writing icing

80 green marzipan leaves

ALSO REQUIRED

40 cake pop sticks

40 small terracotta pots (optional)

YOSHI COOKIES

PREP TIME: 50 MINUTES (INCLUDING RESTING) • COOK TIME: 15 MINUTES (PLUS COOLING)

YOSHI ALWAYS TOPS THE LISTS OF THE CUTEST MARIO CHARACTERS. WITH GOOD REASON: YOSHIS ARE JUST ADORABLE, IN ALL THE MANY DIFFERENT VERSIONS OF THE SPECIES FOUND THROUGHOUT THE MUSHROOM KINGDOM. THESE COOKIES ARE JUST AS IRRESISTIBLE AS YOSHI HIMSELF, AS YOUR FRIENDS AND FAMILY WILL ATTEST! YOU MIGHT WISH YOU HAD A STICKY TONGUE A FEW FEET LONG YOURSELF SO YOU CAN SNAG AT LEAST A COUPLE COOKIES INSTEAD OF COMING AWAY EMPTY-HANDED!

★ ★ ★

1. Combine the flour, sugar, marzipan, butter, egg yolk, baking soda, and cream of tartar in a large bowl and carefully knead together by hand. This requires a fair bit of effort at the start, since the dough will be very crumbly, but as the ingredients come together, so does the dough. The dough is ready when it holds together well. Then wrap in plastic wrap and refrigerate for at least 30 minutes.

2. Meanwhile, preheat the oven to 350°F. Line a baking sheet with parchment paper.

3. Sprinkle the counter with a bit of flour. Use a rolling pin to roll the chilled dough to a ¼-inch thickness. Use a Yoshi-shaped cookie cutter to cut out cookies. Set them on the baking sheet, about 1 inch apart. Knead the dough scraps back together, roll out again, and cut out more Yoshis. You should end up with about 30 cookies.

4. Bake for 12 to 14 minutes, until light brown, then remove the cookies from the oven and leave on the sheet to cool completely.

5. Decorate the cooled Yoshi cookies with the sugar glazes (see image) using piping bags with thin tips. Allow to dry briefly before serving.

MAKES 30 COOKIES

2 cups plus 4 teaspoons flour, plus more for the counter

¼ cup sugar

3.5 ounces marzipan

½ cup (1 stick) plus 3 tablespoons butter, cold

1 egg yolk

¼ teaspoon baking soda

¾ teaspoon cream of tartar

Green, white, red, black, and orange decorating icing, for decorating

ALSO REQUIRED

Yoshi cookie cutter

Piping bags with thin tips

BOB-OMB TRUFFLES

PREP TIME: 10 MINUTES • COOK TIME: 45 MINUTES (INCLUDING COOLING)

IT'S NEVER A GOOD SIGN WHEN A BOB-OMB APPEARS, SINCE A LOUD BOOM IS NEVER FAR OFF.
IT'S BEST TO AVOID THESE WALKING BOMBS WHEN YOU RUN ACROSS THEM IN THE MUSHROOM KINGDOM.
THESE BOB-OMBS ARE JUST THE SWEETEST, THOUGH! WONDERFULLY CHOCOLATEY ON THE OUTSIDE,
WITH A DELICIOUS CREAMY FILLING AND A SAVORY SALTED PRETZEL IN BACK, THESE TRUFFLES TASTE
AS SPECTACULAR AS THEY LOOK. DON'T RUN AWAY, OR YOU'LL BE SORRY!

★ ★ ★

TO MAKE THE TRUFFLES:

1. Line a baking sheet with parchment paper. Melt the chocolate in a double boiler or bain-marie, or by heating in 10-second intervals in the microwave.

2. Combine the melted chocolate, butter, vanilla, heavy cream, and rum (if using) in a medium bowl and stir until smooth. Refrigerate for 15 minutes.

3. Once the mixture has cooled enough that you can work with it easily, scoop it out by teaspoons and shape into balls the size of truffles. Set them on the prepared baking sheet to dry. Once the chocolate has set, use a small, sharp knife to carefully create the vertical pattern (see image).

TO ASSEMBLE:

4. Line a baking sheet with parchment paper. Place the chopped milk and white chocolates in two separate small bowls and melt each in a double boiler or bain-marie, or by heating in 10-second intervals in the microwave. Transfer half of the white chocolate to another small bowl and color slightly with blue food coloring.

5. Using a pastry bag with a fine tip, apply two drops of milk chocolate to each truffle as the "legs" and press a yellow candy into place on each. Allow to set briefly so the "feet" hold on their own, then transfer to the prepared baking sheet to dry. Then use the milk chocolate to apply a mini pretzel to the "back" of each Bob-omb and allow it to dry as well.

6. Fill a second pastry bag with the blue-colored chocolate and add a dollop to the "head" of each truffle. Place a piece of white-chocolate-coated biscuit stick on top as the "fuse" and allow to dry.

7. Finally, fill a third pastry bag with the white chocolate and give each Bob-omb two eyes. (If the chocolate has hardened in the meantime, microwave it again until it is liquid.) Allow to dry one last time.

8. Store the truffles 1 inch apart in airtight containers lined with parchment paper. Important: These truffles aren't as explosive as their namesake, but they are fragile!

MAKES 30 TRUFFLES

TRUFFLES

1¼ cups semisweet chocolate chips

¼ cup (½ stick) butter

1 tablespoon vanilla extract

⅔ cup plus 2 teaspoons heavy cream

Dash rum or Pennsylvania Dutch egg nog (optional)

ASSEMBLY

3 tablespoons milk chocolate, coarsely chopped

3 tablespoons white chocolate, coarsely chopped

2 drops blue paste or gel food coloring

60 yellow small chocolate candies

30 mini salted pretzels

2.5 ounces white-chocolate-coated biscuit sticks, cut into 1-inch pieces

ALSO REQUIRED

3 pastry bags with fine tips

ICE POWER

PREP TIME: 40 MINUTES (INCLUDING RESTING) • COOK TIME: 15 MINUTES

SORBETTI, THE BOSS IN THE FREEZY FLAKE GALAXY IN *SUPER MARIO GALAXY 2* (2010), LOOKS LIKE A SNOWBALL WITH A MEAN FROWN AND A CHERRY-RED NOSE. AND HE'S HUGE—ALMOST AS BIG AS THE PLANETOID HE CALLS HOME. THESE MINI VERSIONS ARE QUITE A BIT SMALLER, AND YOU DON'T HAVE TO MASTER A SPIN ATTACK TO BEAT THEM, EITHER! ALL YOU HAVE TO DO IS POP THESE TASTY SNOWBALLS DOWN THE HATCH, ONE AFTER ANOTHER, AND ENJOY.

★ ★ ★

1. Place all ingredients except the powdered sugar in a large bowl and use your hands or an electric mixer with kneading hook attachments to knead until the dough forms. The dough will be fairly crumbly to start and tend to fall apart when shaped, so cover with plastic wrap and refrigerate for about 20 minutes.

2. Preheat the oven to 350°F. Line a baking sheet with parchment paper.

3. Knead the refrigerated dough by hand on a lightly floured surface. Divide into 40 equal portions, shaping each one into a ball. Place the balls about 1 inch apart on the prepared baking sheet and bake for 12 to 15 minutes until golden.

4. Remove from oven, allow to cool briefly, and place in a large container with a lid. Sift the powdered sugar over the cookies, then place the lid on the container and carefully turn over so all of the cookies are covered on all sides with powdered sugar, resembling snowballs.

5. These cookies will keep two to three weeks in an airtight sealed container.

MAKES 40 COOKIES

4 cups flour, plus more for the counter

1 cup chopped or slivered almonds

5 egg yolks

1⅛ cups (2¼ sticks) butter

1 teaspoon vanilla extract

½ cup granulated sugar

¾ cup powdered sugar

BOWSER'S BIG DONUTS

PREP TIME: 120 MINUTES (INCLUDING RISING AND RESTING TIME) • COOK TIME: 45 MINUTES

DONUTS ARE ALWAYS WELCOME—INCLUDING IN THE MUSHROOM KINGDOM. IN *MARIO & LUIGI: BOWSER'S INSIDE STORY* (2009), FOR EXAMPLE, BOWSER HAS TO TAKE ON MIDBUS AT THE FAWFUL THEATER. WHENEVER MIDBUS HITS BOWSER, THE AUDIENCE CAN THROW A DONUT TO BOWSER AS HE FIGHTS THE BOSS. BOWSER CAN EITHER PUNCH IT AWAY OR EAT IT TO IMMEDIATELY RESTORE HIS STRENGTH. THESE DARK CHOCOLATE DELIGHTS WILL DO MORE THAN JUST LEAVE YOU FEELING SATISFIED AND STRONG. THEY'LL PUT A SMILE ON THE FACE OF EVEN A BAD GUY LIKE BOWSER!

★ ★ ★

1. Combine the flour and yeast in a large bowl.

2. Add the milk, sugar, vanilla extract, butter, egg, and egg yolk, along with a generous pinch of salt. Knead all ingredients together for at least 10 minutes, until a soft, smooth dough forms. Cover the bowl with a clean dish cloth and leave to rise in a warm spot for about 1 hour, until the dough has doubled in size.

3. Roll out the dough to a ½-inch thickness on a lightly floured surface. Use a donut cutter or a similarly sized water glass to cut out donuts. (If you are using a glass to cut out the dough, you will also need a smaller shot glass to cut a hole in the middle of each circle of dough.)

4. Place the donuts about 1 inch apart on a piece of parchment paper. Cover with a clean dish cloth and allow to rest for 20 minutes.

5. While the dough is resting, heat the oil in a large pot over medium heat until the oil reaches 340°F. Working in batches of two to three donuts at a time, add the dough to the hot oil and deep fry for 2 to 3 minutes on each side until golden brown. Use a skimmer or slotted spoon to carefully remove the donuts from the oil and place them on paper towels on a plate to drain and cool a bit.

6. While the donuts are cooling, melt the chocolate in a double boiler or bain-marie (or by heating in short bursts in the microwave). Hold each cooled donut horizontally and dip it halfway into the melted chocolate, allow to drip briefly, then flip over and place the unglazed side on a plate covered with paper towels.

7. Sprinkle the chocolate sprinkles over the donuts while the glaze is still warm and sticky. Allow to dry briefly before serving.

MAKES 12 TO 15 DONUTS

4 cups flour, plus more for the counter

1 package (2¼ teaspoons) active dry yeast

¾ cup plus 1 tablespoon milk, lukewarm

⅜ cup sugar

1 teaspoon vanilla extract

6 tablespoons (¾ stick) butter, at room temperature

1 egg, at room temperature

1 egg yolk

Pinch salt

2 to 3 quarts (8 to 12 cups) oil (depending on pan size), for frying

1¼ cups dark chocolate chips

Chocolate sprinkles, for decoration

ALSO REQUIRED

Donut cutter (3½ inches in diameter); alternatively, use a water glass and a shot glass

CHAIN CHOMP CAKE

PREP TIME: 30 MINUTES • COOK TIME: 30 MINUTES

CHAIN CHOMPS ARE SOME OF THE MOST AGGRESSIVE OPPONENTS IN THE MUSHROOM KINGDOM, TRYING TO BITE ANYTHING THAT COMES NEAR THEM. WITH THIS RECIPE, IT'S THE OTHER WAY AROUND: AS SOON AS YOU GET NEAR THIS CHOCOLATE CHAIN CHOMP CAKE, YOU'LL FEEL AN IRRESISTIBLE URGE TO ATTACK IT AND POLISH IT OFF! BUT DON'T TRY TO GOBBLE DOWN THE CHAIN, TOO, OR YOUR DENTIST WILL BE THE ONLY ONE DELIGHTED WITH THIS CULINARY WORK OF ART!

★ ★ ★

TO MAKE THE CAKE:

1. Preheat the oven to 350°F. Line a 10-inch springform pan with parchment paper.

2. Combine the chocolate and butter in a heat-proof bowl and melt using a double boiler or bain-marie, or by heating in 10-second intervals in the microwave. Remove from the heat and allow to cool briefly.

3. Meanwhile, beat the sugar and eggs with an electric mixer in a separate bowl until creamy.

4. Sift the flour, cocoa, baking soda, and cream of tartar together, then add to the sugar mixture. Combine briefly, then add the chocolate-and-butter mixture and combine. Transfer the batter to the prepared cake pan. Smooth the top and bake for about 30 minutes, or until a toothpick inserted into the middle of the cake comes out clean. Remove from the oven and allow to cool completely before carefully removing it from the springform pan.

TO MAKE THE GANACHE:

5. Meanwhile, in a small pot over medium heat, bring the heavy cream just to a boil. Remove from the heat, add the chocolate, and whisk until the chocolate has melted completely. Allow to cool to the point where the mixture can be spread on.

6. Spread the ganache (not excessively evenly) onto the top and sides of the cooled cake and allow to set. Do not refrigerate, or the fondant will not stick later on!

TO ASSEMBLE:

7. Use a rolling pin to roll out the fondant on the counter, then use a knife to cut out the elements for the eye and mouth with teeth (see image). Then place the fondant in the appropriate spots on the cake and press lightly to adhere.

**MAKES 1 CAKE
(8 to 10 servings)**

CAKE

1 cup chocolate chips or semisweet baking chocolate, coarsely chopped

1⅛ cups (2¼ sticks) butter

½ cup plus 5 teaspoons sugar

5 eggs

2 tablespoons flour

3 tablespoons cocoa powder

¼ teaspoon baking soda

¾ teaspoon cream of tartar

GANACHE AND DECORATION

⅓ cup plus 2 tablespoons heavy cream

½ cup plus 2 tablespoons chocolate chips or semisweet baking chocolate, coarsely chopped

Red, white, and black fondant

ALSO REQUIRED

10-inch springform pan

DIFFICULTY: 🍄🍄

1-UP MUSHROOMS

PREP TIME: 30 MINUTES • COOK TIME: 20 MINUTES

MUSHROOMS ARE AMONG THE MOST COMMON ITEMS FOUND THROUGHOUT THE *SUPER MARIO* SERIES. NORMALLY, 1-UP MUSHROOMS GIVE THE PLAYER AN EXTRA LIFE OR HAVE ANOTHER POSITIVE EFFECT. THESE MUFFINS HAVE MANY BENEFITS, FILLING YOUR BELLY WHILE ALSO FEATURING A CUTE LOOK THAT CHARMS ANYONE WHO SEES THEM. GIVE IT A TRY AND SEE FOR YOURSELF!

★ ★ ★

TO MAKE THE MUFFINS:

1. Preheat the oven to 400°F. Line a muffin pan with muffin liners.

2. Using an electric mixer, beat the eggs in a large bowl until frothy. Then add the milk, butter, sugar, and vanilla extract and beat to combine.

3. Combine the flour, baking soda, cream of tartar, and salt in a separate bowl and slowly mix into the liquid ingredients, using the mixer.

4. Transfer the batter evenly (and very generously, so that the liners are filled to the brim) into the prepared muffin pan and bake for 15 to 20 minutes, or until a toothpick inserted into the center of the muffins comes out clean (even if they are still relatively light in color). Then remove them from the oven and allow to cool before carefully removing from the pan.

TO DECORATE:

5. Use a teaspoon or fork to combine the powdered sugar and milk in a bowl until there are no more visible lumps. Divide evenly among three bowls and color the contents of each with one of the different colors of food coloring. Then either carefully dip the tops of the muffins into the desired glaze or brush it on. Allow to dry for several minutes.

6. Meanwhile, melt the white and milk chocolate in separate bowls over a bain-marie or water bath, or in 10-second intervals in the microwave. Transfer the white chocolate to a pastry bag and dot on as desired to make "muffin mushrooms" (see image). Allow to dry for several minutes.

7. Use the melted milk chocolate to draw two small vertical lines onto each of the paper cups around the muffins. Then, using the pastry bag, draw a small dot of white chocolate onto each line to give the 1-Up Mushrooms their characteristic eyes.

MAKES 12 MUFFINS

MUFFINS

2 eggs

6 tablespoons milk

½ cup (1 stick) plus 1 tablespoon butter, at room temperature

⅔ cup sugar

1 tablespoon vanilla extract

2 cups flour

¼ teaspoon baking soda

¾ teaspoon cream of tartar

Pinch salt

DECORATION

1⅓ cups powdered sugar

4 to 6 tablespoons milk

Green, red, and blue food coloring

3.5 ounces white chocolate, coarsely chopped

Milk chocolate, coarsely chopped

ALSO REQUIRED

Muffin pan

12 paper muffin liners

Pastry bag

103

PRINCESS PEACH CAKE

PREP TIME: 60 MINUTES (PLUS COOLING TIME) • COOK TIME: 75 MINUTES

THE FACT THAT PRINCESS PEACH IS SO POPULAR IN THE MUSHROOM KINGDOM AND BEYOND IS NO COINCIDENCE. SHE'S NOT JUST KIND, GENEROUS, AND OPTIMISTIC, BUT EQUALLY SMART, GRACEFUL, ADVENTUROUS, ELEGANT, AND ALWAYS READY TO GIVE EVERYTHING FOR HER FRIENDS. NOT TO MENTION THAT SHE'S VERY GOOD AT FIGHTING, GO-CARTING, AND DANCING—AND IN THOSE IMPRESSIVE CLOTHES TO BOOT! THAT'S SOMETHING NO ONE CAN IMITATE IN A HURRY. SO LET'S PAY TRIBUTE TO THE PRINCESS WITH THIS CAKE, WHICH IS BRIGHT PINK AND JUST AS SUGARY AS PEACH HERSELF!

★ ★ ★

1. Preheat the oven to 350°F. Place one sheet of parchment paper on the base of each springform pan and clamp into place with the sides of the pan.

TO MAKE THE CAKE:

2. Beat the eggs, sugar, and vanilla extract in a large bowl with an electric mixer set to the highest speed for about 10 minutes, or until the mixture has tripled in volume. Then add the flour, gently folding in with a whisk. Spread the batter evenly in the prepared springform pans so each pan is about half full. Smooth the tops.

3. Bake the two cakes for 30 to 35 minutes each. Remove from the oven when a cake tester comes out clean, and allow to cool for 10 minutes. Guide a bread knife along the edge of the cake base to carefully remove it from the pan and allow to cool completely.

TO MAKE THE GANACHE:

4. Transfer the heavy cream to a small pot over medium heat and bring to a boil, stirring occasionally. Transfer the chocolate to a medium bowl and pour the hot cream over it. Allow to stand for 5 minutes, then stir until the chocolate has melted completely. Set aside to cool to room temperature.

TO MAKE THE FILLING:

5. Soften the gelatin in a bowl of cold water for 10 minutes. Combine 4 tablespoons of the orange juice and the cornstarch in a small bowl. Transfer the remaining orange juice to a small pot, add the sugar, and bring to a boil over medium heat, stirring frequently. Then stir in the cornstarch mixture and bring to a boil again. Remove from the heat and stir in the lemon and orange zest.

MAKES 1 CAKE (10 servings)

CAKE

6 eggs

1 cup sugar

1 tablespoon vanilla extract

1½ cups flour

GANACHE

1¾ cups heavy cream

4⅔ cups chocolate chips or semisweet baking chocolate, coarsely chopped

FILLING

2 sheets gelatin

⅞ cup orange juice, divided

3 tablespoons cornstarch

3 tablespoons plus 1 teaspoon sugar

Zest of ½ lemon

Zest of ½ orange

⅓ cup plus 2 tablespoons heavy cream

⅓ cup plus 1 tablespoon sour cream

ASSEMBLY

3 to 4 tablespoons apricot jam

2 rolls ready-rolled pink fondant, at room temperature

Edible flowers, for topping

ALSO REQUIRED

10-inch springform pan

9-inch springform pan

2 cake rings

Continued on page 106

Continued from page 105

6. Squeeze out the gelatin and stir it into the hot mixture until it has dissolved completely. Allow to cool for several minutes.

7. Beat the heavy cream in a mixing cup until stiff peaks form and refrigerate for several minutes. Once the citrus mixture has cooled, stir in the sour cream, then fold in the whipped cream.

TO ASSEMBLE:

8. Slice both cake bases horizontally into three equal pieces. It is best to divide the filling in half at this point to make sure you have enough for each cake tier.

9. Set one of the 10-inch cake pieces on a serving plate and spread evenly with the jam, leaving a margin of a little under an inch around the edge. Set the second base piece neatly on top and place a cake ring around the two pieces. Spread the filling on the second piece, then top with the last base piece. Repeat this procedure with the 9-inch cake. Refrigerate the two cakes for 1 hour.

10. Spread a thin, even layer of ganache on all sides of the cooled cakes, then refrigerate for another 20 minutes. Then spread with the remaining ganache, smooth on all sides, and refrigerate for another hour.

11. Spread out the ready-rolled fondant on the counter and roll out a bit if necessary. Then carefully place over both cakes, press into place, smooth, and cut away any excess fondant. Finally, place the smaller cake on top of the large one, smooth again, and serve decorated with edible flowers to taste.

WEDDING CAKE

PREP TIME: 60 MINUTES • COOK TIME: 5 MINUTES

BOWSER IS THE KING OF THE KOOPAS—AND HE'S OBSESSED WITH MARRYING PRINCESS PEACH. IT ISN'T MUTUAL, THOUGH, WHICH IS WHY BOWSER IS CONSTANTLY KIDNAPPING PEACH TO DRAG HER TO THE ALTAR BY FORCE. HE'S NOT MUCH OF A GENTLEMAN, OUR BOWSER. BUT WHILE HE MAY BE VILLAINOUS, HE DOES HAVE A SENSE FOR ROMANCE—IN *SUPER MARIO ODYSSEY* (2017), HIS WEDDING OUTFIT IS A SNAZZY WHITE SUIT WITH A PURPLE VEST, HIS WEDDING CAKE IS TOWERING AND FANCY, HIS RING IS *HUGE*, AND THE WEDDING HALL IS DECORATED TO PERFECTION. THIS GLITZY, GLITTERY WEDDING CAKE IS JUST TO HIS TASTE.

★ ★ ★

MAKES 1 CAKE (15 servings)

CREAM FILLING

2 packages chocolate or vanilla pudding mix

4 cups milk, divided

½ cup sugar

¾ cup plus 2 tablespoons heavy cream

1 tablespoon cream of tartar

2 tablespoons vanilla extract

GANACHE

¾ cup plus 2 tablespoons heavy cream

3½ cups white chocolate

ASSEMBLY

3 sponge cake layers, each cut into 3 slices of equal thickness

3 packages white ready-rolled fondant

Edible adhesive

Silver sugar pearls (nonpareils)

White marzipan flowers or real white flowers

Edible glitter

TO MAKE THE CREAM FILLING:

1. Combine the pudding mix with ¾ cup of the milk and the sugar in a bowl. Place the remaining 3¼ cups of milk in a medium pot over medium heat. Bring to a boil, then add the pudding mixture, stir to combine, and return to a boil until thickened. Immediately transfer the pudding mixture to a separate bowl to cool, stirring frequently in the meantime to prevent a skin from forming on the top. Once the pudding is no longer hot, cover securely with plastic wrap directly on the surface. Place in the refrigerator to cool completely.

2. In a large bowl, combine the heavy cream, vanilla extract, and cream of tartar, and beat with an electric mixer on the high setting until stiff peaks form. Fold the whipped cream into the completely cooled pudding.

TO MAKE THE GANACHE:

3. Transfer the heavy cream to a small pot and bring to a brief boil over medium heat. Immediately remove from the heat, add the chocolate, and stir until the chocolate has dissolved completely. Allow to cool for several minutes.

TO ASSEMBLE:

4. Prepare the ready-made cake layers. Three of the layers should be left in their existing size. Neatly stack three others and use a large, sharp knife to cut off about 1¼ inches all the way around the outer edge. Repeat with the last three layers, but this time cut off about 2½ inches. To make your cuts as clean as possible, place a plate of the correct size on the top layer and use it to guide the knife.

5. Place one of the large layers on a serving plate and use a baking spatula to spread the cream filling evenly on top, leaving a bare 1¼-inch border around the edge. Then top with the next layer of the same size, spread with cream filling in the same way, and set the last large layer on top.

Continued on page 108

Continued from page 107

6. Continue reassembling the layers in the same fashion with the medium and small cake layers, until all of the layers and cream filling have been used up and you have three separate cakes of different sizes.

7. Generously coat the cakes on all sides with ganache so the cream filling is "locked in" and will not come into contact with the fondant later on (since the moisture in the cream could cause the fondant to peel away from the cake).

8. Roll out the fondant and place a layer of fondant over each cake. Gently press into place on top and on the sides and carefully smooth. Cut off any excess fondant.

9. Center the medium cake on top of the large cake, then center the small cake on top of the medium one, applying a bit of edible adhesive between the two upper cakes for firmer hold.

10. Finally, decorate the wedding cake with the sugar pearls and marzipan flowers. Sprinkle the entire cake liberally with glitter. Refrigerate until served.

PRINCESS DAISY'S LOVELY APPLE PIE

PREP TIME: 60 MINUTES (INCLUDING RESTING) • COOK TIME: 30 MINUTES

PRINCESS DAISY IS LOVELY AND SWEET HERSELF—JUST LIKE THIS CLASSIC APPLE PIE! MAKING IT IN THE REAL WORLD IS PRETTY DIFFERENT FROM THE PROCESS IN THE MUSHROOM KINGDOM, THOUGH. IN *PAPER MARIO* (2000), FOR EXAMPLE, TAYCE T. ONLY NEEDS TWO INGREDIENTS: AN APPLE AND A CAKE MIX. WE NEED A FEW MORE THINGS TO BAKE OUR VERSION, WHICH WOULD DEFINITELY EARN A COIN OR TWO FROM MARIO AND HIS FRIENDS!

★ ★ ★

TO MAKE THE CRUST:

1. Combine the flour, baking soda, and cream of tartar in a small bowl, then sift into a large bowl. Cut the cold butter into ½-inch cubes and spread evenly over the flour mixture. Add the sugar, vanilla extract, and egg and knead vigorously by hand until a smooth, supple dough forms. Cover the bowl with plastic wrap and refrigerate for 30 minutes.

2. Grease the pie pan with butter.

3. Flour the counter. Take the dough out of the refrigerator and knead again by hand for a few minutes, until the dough is nice and smooth and no longer crumbles or sticks to your fingers. Then divide the dough into two equal portions and use a rolling pin to roll each one out about ½ inch thick. Place one of the dough circles in the greased pan and press into place all around. Using your hands, carefully pull the dough up the sides of the pan, then cut off any excess at the top of the pan. Prick the base all over with a fork.

4. Use a large, sharp knife to slice the second circle of dough into ½-inch-thick strips.

TO MAKE THE FILLING:

5. Peel and core the apples, then cut them into 1-inch cubes.

6. Combine the margarine, sugar, eggs, vanilla extract, flour, baking soda, and cream of tartar in a large bowl and mix with an electric mixer on medium speed for about 2 minutes, until a smooth mixture forms. Carefully fold in the apple using a spatula or spoon.

TO ASSEMBLE:

7. Fill the lined pan evenly with apple filling, then smooth the top and use the strips of dough to form a lattice pattern (see image). Place the lattice on top of the filling. Press into place at the edges and cut off all excess. Brush the lattice with the egg yolk and bake at 350°F for about 30 minutes, until a toothpick inserted into the middle comes out clean. (There is no need to preheat the oven.) If the lattice begins to darken too much during baking, cover with aluminum foil.

8. Remove the pie from the oven and allow to cool completely in the pan. Sprinkle generously with powdered sugar before serving.

MAKES 1 PIE (8 servings)

BASE

1½ cups flour, plus more for the counter

¼ teaspoon baking soda

¾ teaspoon cream of tartar

5 tablespoons cold butter or margarine, plus more to grease the pan

⅓ cup sugar

1 teaspoon vanilla extract

1 egg

FILLING

3 large apples

1 cup (2 sticks) margarine

1 cup sugar

5 eggs

1 teaspoon vanilla extract

3 cups flour

¾ teaspoon baking soda

1½ teaspoon cream of tartar

1 egg yolk, beaten

Powdered sugar

ALSO REQUIRED

8- or 9-inch pie pan or deep tart pan

FIRE FLOWER COOKIES

PREP TIME: 20 MINUTES • COOK TIME: 15 MINUTES

FIRE FLOWERS TURN MARIO INTO FIRE MARIO WHEN HE TOUCHES THEM. IN THIS FORM, HE CAN DO THINGS LIKE SHOOT FIREBALLS FROM HIS HANDS, WHICH VANQUISHES ALMOST ANY ENEMY HE MIGHT RUN ACROSS. THESE COOKIES WON'T MAKE YOU SHOOT FIRE, BUT THEY SURE ARE DELICIOUS! AND YOU DON'T EVEN HAVE TO SMASH A BUNCH OF ? BLOCKS TO GET YOUR HANDS ON THEM—YOU JUST HAVE TO CRACK A COUPLE OF EGGS!

★ ★ ★

1. Combine the flour, cornstarch, sugar, and vanilla extract in a large bowl. Add the butter and egg. Using an electric mixer with kneading hook attachments, knead the ingredients together briefly. Then cover with plastic wrap and refrigerate for 15 minutes.

2. Place the dough on a lightly floured surface and carefully knead with your hands until the dough is no longer sticky. Then divide into four equal portions and color one red, one green, and one yellow with the food coloring.

3. Roll out the red and yellow dough using a rolling pin. Form the uncolored dough into a long, even rope and place it on top of the rolled-out yellow dough. Roll the yellow dough firmly around it and then do the same with the red dough to form a log.

4. Preheat the oven to 350°F on the convection setting, if you have it. Line a baking sheet with parchment paper.

5. Roll out the green dough, cut it into 1½-inch-long "stems," and set the pieces on the baking sheet with generous spacing around all sides. Shape any messy "stems" into small balls and place them to the left and right of the dough stems to form "leaves," then press gently into place.

6. Use a large, sharp knife to cut the dough roll evenly into ¾-inch-thick slices. Place each one at the top of each "stem" as a "flower" and press lightly into place so each cookie looks like a Fire Flower. Bake for about 10 to 12 minutes, or until firm. Remove the cookies from the oven and allow to cool completely on the baking sheets.

7. Meanwhile, melt some of the two kinds of chocolate over a water bath or bain-marie, or in 10-second intervals in the microwave in separate small bowls. Use a toothpick to apply the characteristic eyes to the Fire Flowers (see image). To do this, make two vertical lines of brown chocolate on the uncolored portion of each cookie and allow to dry briefly. Place a dot of white chocolate on each and allow it to dry briefly, as well.

MAKES ABOUT 30 COOKIES

3 cups flour, plus more for the counter

¾ cup plus 2 tablespoons cornstarch

¾ cup sugar

1 tablespoon vanilla extract

½ cup (1 stick) plus 6 tablespoons butter, cut into small pieces

1 egg

Red, green, and yellow gel food coloring

2 to 3 tablespoons milk chocolate chips

1 to 2 tablespoons white chocolate chips

BOO SUGAR COOKIES

PREP TIME: 40 MINUTES • COOK TIME: 10 MINUTES

EVERYONE KNOWS THERE'S A LOT OF FUNNY BUSINESS GOING ON IN THE MUSHROOM KINGDOM. BUT EVEN BY THE STANDARDS OF THE MARIO UNIVERSE, THE BOOS ARE PRETTY ODD LITTLE FELLOWS, SINCE THESE GHOSTS SEEM TO BE MORE FRIGHTENED OF YOU THAN THE OTHER WAY AROUND WHEN YOU FIRST ENCOUNTER THEM. BUT ONCE THEY GET OVER THEIR SHYNESS, THEY'RE JUST WAITING FOR YOU TO TURN YOUR BACK SO THEY CAN REALLY HOUND YOU. SCARY, ISN'T IT? THESE COOKIE "GHOSTS" ARE ONE THING ABOVE ALL: DELICIOUS. AND THEY AREN'T SCARY AT ALL! (WELL, MAYBE A LITTLE.)

★ ★ ★

1. In a large bowl, combine the flour, butter, sugar, vanilla extract, and egg and knead carefully by hand until the heat of your hands (and your hard work) forms a nice, smooth dough. Wrap the dough in plastic wrap and refrigerate for 30 minutes.

2. Preheat the oven to 400°F. Line a baking sheet with parchment paper.

3. Knead the chilled dough again, use a rolling pin to roll it out thinly on a lightly floured surface, then use a 3-inch round cookie cutter (or, alternatively, a similar-sized glass) to cut out circular shapes. Set them about 1 inch apart on the prepared baking sheet. You should have about 30 cookies.

4. Knead the rest of the dough again and shape it into pea-size balls. Press these balls flat and shape them so you can place them on the left and right of the Boos to form arms (see image). Press the arms into place so they connect with the circles of dough.

5. Bake for about 10 minutes, or until the cookies are pale yellow. Remove the cookies and allow to cool on the baking sheet.

6. Meanwhile, use an electric mixer to combine the powdered sugar and egg whites in a medium bowl until the sugar has completely dissolved and the mixture has formed a sticky, shiny glaze. Place 4 tablespoons of glaze in a small bowl, then place 4 more tablespoons in a second small bowl. Color one with the black food coloring and the other with red. Then transfer all three glazes (white, red, black) to separate pastry bags with thin tips.

7. Coat the cooled cookies evenly with white glaze, leaving some space around the edge on all sides. Allow to dry briefly. Then use the black and red glaze to draw on the mouth and eyes. Allow to dry briefly again.

8. Store the cookies in an airtight container so they stay nice and scary (and don't dry out).

MAKES 30 COOKIES

1⅔ cups flour, plus more for the counter

5 tablespoons butter, cold

⅜ cup sugar

1 tablespoon vanilla extract

1 egg

2⅔ cups powdered sugar

2 egg whites

Few drops black and red gel or paste food coloring

ALSO REQUIRED

3-inch round cookie cutter

3 pastry bags with thin tips

DIFFICULTY: 🍄🍄

PRINCESS-WORTHY HANAMI DANGO

PREP TIME: 30 MINUTES • COOK TIME: 15 MINUTES

PRINCESS PEACH TOADSTOOL (YES, THAT'S REALLY HER FULL NAME!) IS THE RULER OF THE MUSHROOM KINGDOM AND MARIO'S TRUE LOVE. AND NO WONDER: APART FROM HER SMARTNESS, CLEVERNESS, KINDNESS, AND GRACE (EVEN IN HIGH HEELS!), SHE IS BEAUTIFUL—JUST LIKE THESE DANGOS, A JAPANESE SWEET IN COLORS INSPIRED BY PEACH'S CROWN. IT DOESN'T GET MUCH MORE ROYAL THAN THIS!

★ ★ ★

1. Combine the two types of rice flour in a large bowl. Gradually add the water, then the sugar, and use your hands to work into a firm, smooth dough. Use a knife to cut the dough into three equal pieces.

2. Combine one of the pieces of dough with the spirulina powder and knead carefully. Carefully color the second piece of dough with the raspberry juice and knead thoroughly so the color is evenly distributed. Knead the turmeric into the third piece of dough. If the dough feels dry to the touch, moisten your fingers, which will help to knead some water into the dough. (If the pieces of dough are not vivid enough in color, add a drop or two of red, blue, or yellow food coloring to each.)

3. Shape each piece of dough into a long rope, cut in half, and divide each half into six equal-sized pieces. Shape each piece of dough into a nice ball between the palms of your hands so you have 12 balls of each color.

4. Fill a bowl with cold water.

5. Bring 2 quarts (64 fluid ounces) of water to a boil in a large pot over medium heat. Once the water boils, carefully add the balls of the first color and simmer until the dangos rise to the surface on their own (about 5 minutes). Then use a skimmer or slotted spoon to remove the dangos from the pot, briefly immerse them in the cold water, and set on paper towels on a plate to drain. Repeat with the balls in the other two colors.

6. Once all of the dangos are cooked and have cooled a bit, arrange on a skewer in the following order: red, yellow, blue. Serve promptly at room temperature.

MAKES 12 SKEWERS

⅔ cup plus 2 teaspoons sticky (glutinous) rice flour

⅔ cup plus 2 teaspoons rice flour

¾ cup water

3 tablespoons sugar

1 to 2 tablespoons blue spirulina powder

2 to 3 tablespoons raspberry juice

1 to 2 tablespoons turmeric

Red, blue, and yellow food coloring (optional)

ALSO REQUIRED

12 wooden skewers (6 to 8 inches long)

YOSHI'S COOKIE EGGS

PREP TIME: 40 MINUTES (INCLUDING RESTING) • COOK TIME: 30 MINUTES (PLUS COOLING)

YOSHI IS ONE OF THE MUSHROOM KINGDOM'S BIGGEST HEROES, NOT LEAST BECAUSE HE HAS HELPED HIS FRIEND MARIO VANQUISH BOWSER MANY TIMES OVER. YOSHI BELONGS TO THE SPECIES OF THE SAME NAME, WHICH IS KNOWN FOR ITS FLUTTERING FLIGHT PATTERN AND EXTREMELY LONG TONGUE, WHICH THEY CAN USE TO DO THINGS LIKE GRAB ENEMIES OR ITEMS FROM A DISTANCE. ASIDE FROM THAT, YOSHIS ARE JUST AMAZINGLY CUTE! AND THEY HATCH FROM EGGS—ALTHOUGH I DON'T THINK YOU'LL BE ABLE TO RESIST THESE MARVELOUS TREATS LONG ENOUGH TO HATCH ANYTHING FROM THEM.

★ ★ ★

1. Combine the flour, sugar, orange flavoring, butter, egg yolk, baking soda, and cream of tartar in a bowl and carefully knead together by hand until a smooth dough forms. Wrap in plastic wrap and refrigerate for at least 30 minutes.

2. Meanwhile, preheat the oven to 350°F. Line a baking sheet with parchment paper.

3. Sprinkle the counter with a bit of flour. Use a rolling pin to roll the chilled dough to a ¼-inch thickness. Use an egg-shaped cookie cutter to cut out cookies. Set them on the baking sheet, about 1 inch apart. Knead the dough scraps back together, roll out again, and cut out more eggs. You should end up with about 30 cookies.

4. Bake for 12 to 14 minutes, until light brown, then remove the cookies from the oven and leave on the sheet to cool completely.

5. Brush the cooled eggs evenly on one side with the white sugar glaze, leaving a margin to all sides (see image). Apply three green circles to each Yoshi egg while the white glaze is still wet. Allow to dry briefly before serving.

MAKES 30 COOKIES

2½ cups flour, plus more for the counter

⅜ cup sugar

3 to 4 drops orange flavoring (or other flavoring as desired)

½ cup (1 stick) plus 3 tablespoons butter, cold

1 egg yolk

¼ teaspoon baking soda

¾ teaspoon cream of tartar

White and green decorating icing

ALSO REQUIRED

Egg-shaped cookie cutter

WHACKA BUMPS

PREP TIME: 100 MINUTES (INCLUDING RISING) • COOK TIME: 15 MINUTES (PLUS COOLING)

LIFE IS TOUGH FOR A WHACKA IN THE MUSHROOM KINGDOM. YOU SPEND ALL DAY LURKING UNDERGROUND, DIGGING TUNNELS IN TOTAL DARKNESS, AND THEN, WHEN YOU DO FINALLY MAKE YOUR WAY UP TO THE SURFACE FOR A BREATH OF FRESH AIR, YOU GET SMACKED IN THE HEAD, SINCE EVERYONE IS OUT FOR WHACKA BUMP, THE ITEM THAT WHACKAS DROP. IN FACT, WHACKAS HAVE BEEN HUNTED TO NEAR EXTINCTION BECAUSE OF IT, SO WE DECIDED TO MAKE THESE "BUMPS" WITHOUT ANY WHACKAS AT ALL. INSTEAD, FLOUR, YEAST, MILK, AND A COUPLE OF EGGS ARE ALL THAT BITE THE DUST.

TO MAKE THE SHORTBREAD DOUGH:

1. In a large bowl, combine the butter and sugar and beat with an electric mixer until light and creamy. Then add the egg and beat thoroughly to combine.

2. In a separate bowl, combine the flour, baking soda, and cream of tartar. Sift over the butter and egg mixture and use your fingers to combine until it resembles coarse crumbs. Then knead everything together a few times, wrap in plastic wrap, and refrigerate for at least 30 minutes.

TO MAKE THE DOUGH:

3. Sift the flour into a large bowl. Add the dry yeast and the 2 tablespoons of sugar and combine thoroughly.

4. Make a hollow in the center of the flour mixture. Add the egg and milk to the hollow and use an electric mixer with kneading hook attachments on the highest setting to combine until smooth, gradually adding in the flour in the process. Then add the butter and knead the dough for 5 minutes, until it is nice and elastic.

5. Sprinkle flour over the counter, place the yeast dough on top of it, and cover with a clean, damp dish cloth. Allow to rise at room temperature for 1 hour.

6. Press the risen dough lightly with your hands to flatten it slightly and cut it into six equal pieces. Shape each one into a ball, cover again with the cloth, and allow to rise for another 10 minutes.

TO MAKE THE WHACKA BUMPS:

7. Take the shortbread dough out of the refrigerator and knead thoroughly by hand. Form it into a long roll and cut it into six equal pieces. Lightly flour a work surface. Use a rolling pin to roll out each piece into a 4-inch circle.

8. Place a ball of yeast dough in the center of each shortbread circle. Wrap the shortbread around the dough balls so that the tops and sides are covered, but the bottom remains free.

MAKES 6 ROLLS

SHORTBREAD DOUGH

¼ cup (½ stick) butter, at room temperature

¼ cup sugar

1 egg

1 cup all-purpose or bread flour

⅛ teaspoon baking soda

⅓ teaspoon cream of tartar

YEAST DOUGH

2 cups plus 4 teaspoons all-purpose or bread flour, plus more for the counter

2 teaspoons active dry yeast

2 tablespoons sugar, plus ¼ cup sugar for rolling

1 egg

⅜ cup milk

1½ tablespoons salted butter, at room temperature

9. Put the remaining ¼ cup of sugar in a bowl and firmly press the shortbread dough side of the roll into it so that side of the bun is covered with sugar. Then use a pastry scraper or bread knife to press a crosshatch pattern into the top side. Be careful to cut only lightly into the dough. The rolls will rise during baking, and if you make your cuts too deep, they could end up with unsightly bulges!

10. Line a baking sheet with parchment paper. Set the rolls on the prepared baking sheet and allow to rise for 30 minutes. Shortly before the end of the rising time, preheat the oven to 425°F.

11. Bake the rolls on the middle rack for 8 minutes. Then adjust the temperature to 350°F and bake for another 5 minutes, until golden. Remove from the oven and allow to cool completely on the baking sheet or a cooling rack.

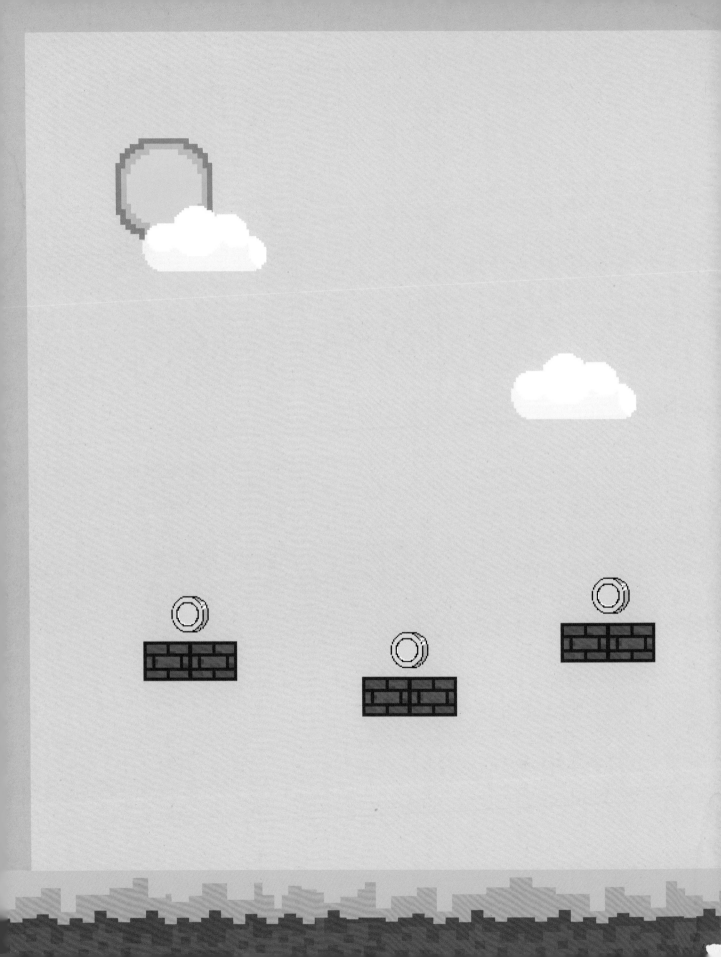

DRINKS

SPECIAL SHAKE

PREP TIME: 5 MINUTES

THE SPECIAL SHAKE IN *PAPER MARIO* (2000) IS PREPARED BY THE COOK TAYCE T. BUT FIRST, YOU HAVE TO BRING HER A LIME AND A MELON OR A JAMMIN' JELLY. FUN FACT: THIS DRINK IS A PRIME EXAMPLE OF THE FACT THAT THE FRUITS OF YOUR LABORS CAN SOMETIMES BE WORSE THAN THE INGREDIENTS THAT GO INTO THEM. AFTER ALL, A JAMMIN' JELLY ON ITS OWN WILL REGENERATE A WHOPPING 50 FLOWER POINTS, BUT ENJOYING A SPECIAL SHAKE YIELDS ONLY 20 FP, SO IT'S BETTER TO MIX LIME AND MELON INSTEAD. IN THIS VERSION OF THE DRINK, WE'VE CREATED A PUNCH OF LIME AND CITRUS, SOMETHING THAT WILL PACK 100 FP IN TERMS OF FRESHNESS AND FLAVOR!

★ ★ ★

1. Place a few ice cubes in two highball glasses and pour half of the liqueur and orange juice into each. Add a squeeze of lime juice to each glass.
2. Slowly pour half of the sparkling water into each glass and stir so the blue liqueur and orange juice combine to make the shake turn green.
3. Garnish with a slice of star fruit to serve.

MAKES 2 SHAKES

Ice cubes

3 fluid ounces alcohol-free blue Curaçao liqueur

1⅜ cups orange juice

2 squeezes lime juice

⅞ cup sparkling water

2 slices star fruit, for garnish

ALSO REQUIRED

2 highball glasses

TIP Want a little more zing in your Special Shake? If you're old enough, feel free to substitute the same amount of sparkling wine for the sparkling water.

TOAD'S TASTY TONIC

PREP TIME: 5 MINUTES

TASTY TONIC HAS A VARIETY OF USES, INCLUDING HEALING THE POISON STATUS EFFECT, WHICH IS WHY IT'S ESPECIALLY HANDY FOR FIGHTING "TOXIC" ENEMIES LIKE POKEY MUMMIES AND PUTRID PIRANHAS. THIS DRINK CAN ALSO BE BOUGHT AT THE ITEM SHOP IN YOSHI'S VILLAGE, BUT WE MAKE OUR TASTY TONIC OURSELVES, OF COURSE, JUST LIKE TAYCE T., WHO USES A LIME, LEMON, BLUE BERRY, OR COCONUT TO MAKE HER VERSION. THIS RECIPE USES SLIGHTLY DIFFERENT INGREDIENTS, AND DRINKING IT WON'T HEAL ANY POISONS, BUT IT'S A REFRESHING DRINK EVEN WITHOUT ADDING ANY HONEY SYRUP!

★ ★ ★

1. Add a few ice cubes to each of two tumblers.
2. Cut the grapefruit slices in half and add two halves to each glass.
3. Pour half of the grapefruit juice and lime juice into each glass, then fill with the tonic water. Stir briefly.
4. Garnish with a rosemary sprig and serve.

MAKES 2 DRINKS

Ice cubes

2 slices grapefruit

⅜ cup grapefruit juice

4 teaspoons lime juice

1¼ cups tonic water

2 sprigs fresh rosemary, for garnish

ALSO REQUIRED

2 tumblers

SUPER SODA

PREP TIME: 5 MINUTES

SUPER SODA IS A KIND OF MAGIC POTION. IT CAN HEAL THE POISON AND TINY STATUS EFFECTS, BUT THAT'S NOT ALL. IT ALSO REGENERATES FLOWER POINTS. YOU CAN BUY SUPER SODA, FIND IT IN SHY GUY'S TOY BOX, OR HAVE IT MADE BY TAYCE T., USING HONEY SYRUP AND A BERRY. TO MAKE THIS SPECIFIC VERSION, THOUGH, YOU'LL NEED DIFFERENT INGREDIENTS, SUCH AS ORANGE JUICE, ALCOHOL-FREE BLUE CURAÇAO, AND STRAWBERRY SYRUP. THIS COLORFUL LAYERED COCKTAIL IS TRUE EYE CANDY, BUT THAT'S NOT ALL. IT'S ALSO A VERITABLE EXPLOSION OF FLAVOR—WITHOUT ANY BOB-OMBS INVOLVED!

★ ★ ★

1. Pour the orange juice into the glass.
2. Hold the glass at an angle and slowly pour the strawberry syrup into the glass (ideally over the back of a spoon) along the inside of the glass so the syrup sinks to the bottom of the glass due to the liquids' difference in density. Allow to stand briefly.
3. In the meantime, combine the liqueur and sparkling water in a small measuring cup.
4. Carefully pour the blue-colored sparkling water into the glass over the back of a spoon, which forms the top colored layers.
5. Garnish with the lemon slice and serve immediately.

MAKES 1 SUPER SODA

⅞ cup orange juice

8 teaspoons strawberry syrup

4 teaspoons alcohol-free blue Curaçao liqueur

½ cup sparkling water

1 slice lemon, for garnish

ALSO REQUIRED

Cocktail glass

SUPER STAR LEMON-LIME SODA

PREP TIME: 10 MINUTES (PLUS 3 HOURS FOR CHILLING)

**STARS ARE ENCHANTING BY NATURE, AND THAT'S EVEN MORE TRUE OF THE STARS IN
THE MUSHROOM KINGDOM, WHICH ALWAYS HAVE A POSITIVE EFFECT ON MARIO AND HIS FRIENDS.
THE SAME GOES FOR THIS SUPER STAR SODA, WITH ITS REFRESHING AND REVITALIZING FLAVOR.
THIS DRINK REALLY PACKS A CITRUSY PUNCH TO GET YOU GOING!**

★ ★ ★

1. Rinse the lemons and limes in hot water and pat dry with paper towels.

2. Slice two of the lemons and two of the limes into slices a little less than ½ inch thick.

3. Juice the remaining lemons and limes and transfer the juice to a large measuring cup. Add the sugar and carefully mix with the juice. Add the lemon and lime slices, cover the cup loosely with plastic wrap, and refrigerate for 3 hours so the flavors can meld.

4. To serve, transfer to a large pitcher, add the lemon balm, and ice cubes to taste, and fill with the sparkling water. Stir briefly and enjoy promptly.

**MAKES ABOUT
50 FLUID OUNCES SODA**

9 lemons

5 limes

1 cup sugar

5 sprigs fresh lemon balm, leaves only

Ice cubes

1 quart (32 fluid ounces) ice-cold sparkling water

ALSO REQUIRED

Juicer

Large pitcher (large enough to hold 50 fluid ounces)

YOSHI'S LASSI

PREP TIME: 20 MINUTES (INCLUDING COOLING)

LASSI IS AN INDIAN YOGURT DRINK. IT IS OFTEN SERVED WITH SPICY FOODS, SINCE THE FAT CONTENT TEMPERS THE HEAT. MANY DIFFERENT KINDS OF LASSI ARE FOUND AROUND ASIA AND EASTERN EUROPE—AND AT THE SUPER NINTENDO WORLD AMUSEMENT PARK IN JAPAN, WHERE VARIOUS FLAVORS ARE AVAILABLE AT YOSHI'S SNACK ISLAND. WITH THAT AS INSPIRATION, HERE IS OUR VERSION WITH MANGO AND MELON, WITH A COLOR THAT PAYS TRIBUTE TO EVERYONE'S FAVORITE YOSHI. THIS DRINK IS AS SWEET AS THE LOVELY PRINCESS PEACH, SO WE ADD A PINCH OF MATCHA POWDER SO THAT YOU DON'T GET A SUGAR SHOCK FROM ALL THE SWEETNESS!

★ ★ ★

1. Peel the mangoes with a sharp knife or vegetable peeler. Cut into large pieces and remove the pit. Cut out 12 nice and evenly sized mango cubes (about 1¼ inches on a side) and set aside. Chop the remaining mango pieces a bit smaller and place in a blender.

2. Add the yogurt, milk, honey, lemon juice, and matcha powder and blend all ingredients together, until you no longer see any pieces and the lassi is smooth and creamy (alternatively, use an immersion blender). Refrigerate for 10 minutes before enjoying.

3. While the lassi is cooling, place three mango cubes on each wooden skewer.

4. Divide the chilled mango lassi among four glasses, sprinkle a pinch of matcha powder over each, and garnish with a mango skewer. Serve promptly.

MAKES 4 SERVINGS

2 mangoes

1 cup Greek yogurt

½ cup milk

2 teaspoons honey

2 tablespoons lemon juice

½ cup matcha powder plus more for garnish

ALSO REQUIRED

4 small wooden skewers

MOO MOO MEADOWS CHOCOLATE

PREP TIME: 20 MINUTES • COOK TIME: 10 MINUTES

IN THE MUSHROOM KINGDOM, MOO MOOS ARE FOUND PRIMARILY IN THE MOO MOO MEADOWS AND AT MOO MOO FARM, WHERE THEY SEEM TO HAVE AN UNERRING INSTINCT FOR TROTTING INTO THE MIDDLE OF THE ROAD AS IF THEY JUST KNOW YOU'LL SPIN OUT IF YOU DRIVE YOUR KART INTO THEM AT FULL SPEED. WHICH, OF COURSE, CAN BE FUN—JUST LIKE THIS DELICIOUS CHOCOLATE DRINK THAT YOU'LL GLADLY TAKE A DETOUR FOR!

★ ★ ★

1. Melt the chocolate, either using a double boiler or bain-marie, or heating in 10-second intervals in the microwave. Once the chocolate is melted, pour a small amount onto the inside of a milkshake glass, then tilt and move the glass around to produce a "cloud" shape. Allow to dry for a few minutes, then follow the same steps to produce the next "clouds." Repeat with a second glass.

2. In a mixing cup, use an electric mixer set to high to beat the heavy cream until stiff peaks form. Set aside.

3. In a small pot over medium heat, heat the milk, cocoa powder, vanilla extract, and chocolate, stirring constantly, until the chocolate is fully melted. Be sure to keep the milk from boiling! Adjust the heat as needed.

4. Remove from heat and allow to cool for 2 to 3 minutes. Mix thoroughly again to combine, then divide evenly between the prepared glasses. Stir briefly. Garnish with whipped cream as desired, then sprinkle with mini marshmallows and drizzle with caramel sauce. Serve immediately.

MAKES 2 SERVINGS

⅛ to ¼ cup dark chocolate

¼ cup heavy cream

2 cups milk

2 tablespoons unsweetened cocoa powder

1 teaspoon vanilla extract

½ cup chocolate chips or semisweet baking chocolate, coarsely chopped

Colorful mini marshmallows, for garnish

Caramel sauce

ALSO REQUIRED

2 tall milkshake glasses

FLOTSAM FLOATS

PREP TIME: 5 MINUTES

FLOTSAMS BELONG MORE IN *DONKEY KONG COUNTRY 2*'S CROCODILE ISLE THAN IN THE MUSHROOM KINGDOM, BUT SINCE THESE STINGRAY-LIKE CREATURES MAKE A BRIEF CAMEO APPEARANCE IN *SUPER MARIO-KUN* (1990) (AND ARE JUST TOTALLY COOL), THEY DESERVE AN HONORABLE MENTION HERE. MOST OF THEM ARE GREEN OR BLUE. WE'VE GONE ONE STEP FURTHER WITH THIS PINK VERSION IN HONOR OF PRINCESS PEACH, WHO WOULD SURELY ENJOY THIS VANILLA ICE CREAM FLOAT WITH DELICIOUS PEACH FLAVORING.

★ ★ ★

TO MAKE THE MELON VERSION:

1. Place a large scoop of ice cream in the bottom of a tall glass.

2. Fill a tall glass with the melon soda up to about two finger widths (about 2 inches) from the brim. Add the green food coloring and stir with a long spoon.

3. Generously top with whipped topping and garnish with the raspberry. Serve immediately.

TO MAKE THE PEACH VERSION:

1. Place a large scoop of ice cream in the bottom of a tall glass.

2. Fill a tall glass with the peach soda up to about two finger widths (about 2 inches) from the brim. Add the heavy cream and red food coloring and gently stir with a long spoon.

3. Generously top with whipped topping and garnish with the peach. Serve immediately.

MAKES 1 SERVING EACH

MELON VERSION

1 large scoop vanilla ice cream

1 melon soda, cold

1 drop green food coloring

Canned whipped topping

1 fresh raspberry

PEACH VERSION

1 large scoop vanilla ice cream

1 peach soda, cold

1 tablespoon heavy cream

1 drop red food coloring

Canned whipped topping

1 peach wedge

ALSO REQUIRED

Tall glass

KOOPA TEA

PREP TIME: 10 MINUTES • COOK TIME: 3 HOURS, 10 MINUTES (INCLUDING DRYING)

TEA IS A GREAT THING. IT WARMS YOU, STRENGTHENS YOU, AND HEALS YOU WHEN YOU'RE NOT FEELING
WELL. IT'S ALWAYS GOOD TO HAVE TEA ON HAND—IN REAL LIFE AS WELL AS IN THE MUSHROOM KINGDOM!
IN THE *PAPER MARIO* SERIES, TAYCE T., ZESS T., AND SAFFRON PREPARE KOOPA TEA IF YOU BRING THEM A
KOOPA LEAF, WHICH YOU GET BY DEFEATING A PAPER KOOPA—A TRICKY PROPOSITION, DEFINITELY.
MAKING THIS TASTY SWEET FRUIT TEA IS CHILD'S PLAY BY COMPARISON.
YOU CAN ALSO STICK WITH THE THEME AND DRINK IT OUT OF A MARIO MUG!

★ ★ ★

1. Rinse the clementines in hot water, then dry with paper towels, peel, and dice finely.

2. Line a baking sheet with parchment paper. Spread the diced clementine, mint, lemon verbena, and mixed flowers evenly across the prepared baking sheet. Either allow to dry in a warm, dry place for several days or dry in the oven for about 3 hours at 150°F. Insert the handle of a wooden spoon into the oven door so the door stays open a crack and the steam generated inside can escape. Then carefully pick the fruit pieces and petals off the paper and dispose of the rest.

3. Using a mortar and pestle, coarsely grind the dried herbs and clementine.

4. In a small bowl, combine the grated licorice and vanilla bean with the black tea. Add the ground herbs and fruit and mix thoroughly.

5. To prepare the tea, place 4 to 5 teaspoons in a tea ball or reusable tea bag and suspend inside a teapot. Pour hot (not boiling!) water over the mixture and steep for 4 to 6 minutes, depending on how strong you like your tea. Then remove the tea ball/bag and serve immediately. It is best to pour the tea through a fine mesh to make sure no residue gets into the teacups.

6. Sweeten with honey to taste (if using).

4 TO 5 POTS OF TEA

2 clementines

1 sprig fresh mint

1 sprig fresh lemon verbena

Handful fresh mixed edible flowers (such as elderflower, mallow, marigold)

1 tablespoon grated licorice root

1 vanilla bean, finely chopped

3.5 ounces black tea

Honey (optional)

ALSO REQUIRED

Mortar and pestle

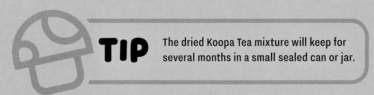

TIP The dried Koopa Tea mixture will keep for several months in a small sealed can or jar.

CONVERSION CHARTS

VOLUME

U.S.	Metric
⅕ teaspoon (tsp)	1 ml
1 teaspoon (tsp)	5 ml
1 tablespoon (tbsp)	15 ml
1 fluid ounce (fl. oz.)	30 ml
⅕ cup	50 ml
¼ cup	60 ml
⅓ cup	80 ml
3.4 fluid ounces (fl. oz.)	100 ml
½ cup	120 ml
⅔ cup	160 ml
¾ cup	180 ml
1 cup	240 ml
1 pint (2 cups)	480 ml
1 quart (4 cups)	.95 liter

TEMPERATURES

Fahrenheit	Celsius
200°F	93.3°C
212°F	100°C
250°F	120°C
275°F	135°C
300°F	150°C
325°F	165°C
350°F	177°C
400°F	205°C
450°F	233°C
475°F	245°C
500°F	260°C

WEIGHT

U.S.	Metric
0.5 ounce (oz.)	14 g
1 ounce (oz.)	28 g
¼ pound (lb.)	113 g
⅓ pound (lb.)	151 g
½ pound (lb.)	227 g
1 pound (lb.)	454 g

ACKNOWLEDGMENTS

Although I'm not much of a fan of florid and long-winded thanks (ahem), no one produces any book entirely on their own—much less a book like this one! This has ended up being one of the most ambitious cookbook projects I've ever tackled.

All that makes me even prouder of this, the product of our collective efforts. The following people (in no particular order) were instrumental in bringing this book to fruition: Dimitrie Harder, my "partner in crime," who brought all my crazy ideas to life in images that keep springing to mind; Jo Löffler and Holger ("Holle") Wiest, my "old hands," without whom nothing would be the same, even after all these years; Ulrich "Pestilence" Peste, my best friend; Thomas Böhm, my "brother from another mother"; Dimitri Keilbach; Katharina "the one and only cat" Böhm; Dennis Winkler; Mareike Kress; Thomas and Alexandra Stamm; the team at Reel Ink Press; and last but not least, my family, rough edges and all.

Feel free to thank these people for everything you like about this book. As for any slips, inaccuracies, or excessive use of celery salt, I take full responsibility.

T. G.

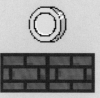

ABOUT THE AUTHOR
AND THE PHOTOGRAPHER

TOM GRIMM

Tom Grimm, born in 1972, apprenticed as a bookseller and has been working ever since as an author, translator, screenwriter, journalist, editor, and producer for a number of international publishers. Alongside his enthusiasm for literature, movies, and video games, he especially enjoys amusement parks, travel, listening to Rammstein, good food, bad jokes, and firing up the grill year-round. He is a passionate amateur cook, although not much of a baker. Even so, he has managed to win the Gourmand World Cookbook Award and other distinctions for his work. Tom lives with his family, a literal pride of cats, and several life-size images of Batman, Kung Fu Panda, Rayman, and Thrall the Orc. He lives and works in a small town in the west of Germany that is really and truly nothing to write home about. (Not kidding. Really.)

DIMITRIE HARDER

Dimitrie "Dimi" Harder was born in what is now the Central Asian country of Kyrgyzstan in 1977, the second child of a Russian mother and a German father. His home country is known for not only its magnificent mountain vistas and spectacular natural settings but also its cultural traditions of myths and sagas. Dimi moved to Germany with his family in 1990. It was here, in his newfound home, that he discovered his passion for photography, eventually turning what had been a hobby into a full-time job after stints as a melon picker, movie projectionist, pizza baker, and construction worker, among other jobs. With great patience and attention to detail, Dimi immerses himself in the mood and atmosphere befitting the worlds where he works with his images. He loves bicycling, running, hiking, and his motorcycle, detests food waste, and is the only person on earth ever to have officially referred to his "partner in crime," Tom Grimm, as a bully. (Which he definitely isn't—it's just that Tom can have a pretty big mouth at times!)

PO Box 15
Cobb, CA 95426

ISBN: 978-1-958862-06-3

Created by Grinning Cat Productions

Written by Tom Grimm

Photography: Tom Grimm & Dimitrie Harder
Typesetting, Cover & Layout: Dennis Winkler
English Translation: Kate Partlan
Copy Editing: Jessica Easto
Author and Photographer Icons: Angelos Tsirigotis

Special thanks to Roberts Urlovskis!

Manufactured in China

10 9 8 7 6 5 4 3 2 1